DAVID
WORSHIPED
A LIVING GOD

DAVID WORSHIPED A LIVING GOD

by

Judson Cornwall, Th.D.

Revival Press
Worship and Praise Division
of
Destiny Image Publishers
P.O. Box 351
Shippensburg, PA 17257

ISBN 0-938612-38-7
Library of Congress Catalog Card Number 89-60663

For Worldwide Distribution
Printed in the U.S.A.

First Printing: 1989
Second Printing: 1993

Destiny Image books are available through these fine distributors outside the United States:

Christian Growth, Inc.
Jalan Kilang-Timor, Singapore 0315

Lifestream
Nottingham, England

Rhema Ministries Trading
Randburg, South Africa

Salvation Book Centre
Petaling, Jaya, Malaysia

Successful Christian Living
Capetown, Rep. of South Africa

Vision Resources
Ponsonby, Auckland, New Zealand

WA Buchanan Company
Geebung, Queensland, Australia

Word Alive
Niverville, Manitoba, Canada

Acknowledgments

None of us lives in a vacuum, nor are we able to work totally alone. Every time I begin a book, I know others will be deeply involved in the task.

If I were only a writer, my wife would not find my writing as competitive; but writing is what I do in my "spare" time, which usually means taking the time we would normally share together to sit in front of my computer. I want to express my humble thanks to my wife, Eleanor, for the years of understanding she has exhibited during my writing tasks. She has especially helped me in the writing of this, my twentieth book.

My earnest thanks also to my secretary, Terri Gargis, who cheerfully accepted the hours of labor this book entailed, although it added to an already heavy work load.

Dedication

To the staff and workers at **T L C** in Scottsdale, Arizona. Faithful worshipers, workers and witnesses to Christian leaders across the nation, they, like David, have learned to live their worship.

Contents

Contents

Preface

I sat recently with a minister who has gained much national attention for his ministry. He was full of questions, most of which indicated that his faith was severely shaken. I knew him years ago when he ministered with a vibrant faith of joy and conviction. Within the past few years, his ministry has kept him involved with the sins of society and its incumbent tragedies. In his efforts to get the Church involved in eradicating some of this social iniquity, he has taken his eyes off the Christ Who called him and has riveted his gaze onto the enormous need of the hour.

It hurt me to hear him admit that he was joyless, discouraged, questioning his faith, and had lost his song. When I spoke to him about Jesus, he responded, "Which Jesus?" and then pointed out that individuals were creating their own concepts of Christ to accommodate their personal desires. After dealing with so many conflicting images, he wondered Who God actually was. Through his involvement with the diverse branches of religion, he had lost contact with the Christ of divine revelation. I seriously doubt that this man stands alone in his inner conflict. His uniqueness is in his willingness to talk about it.

One of the curses of organized religion is the tendency to keep people so actively involved in peripherals that they lose sight of the Person of the Gospels. Service is necessary, but when we become so involved in the service of God that we have lost contact with God Himself, we have made a deadly substitution. Enthusiasm of performance can never take the place of enjoying the Presence of God. When *doing* replaces *being,* our faith is already in jeopardy.

The Mary/Martha syndrome still exists in the Church. Some persons dedicate themselves to be workers, while others feel called to be worshipers. This is inconsistent with the statement of Jesus in the hour of His temptation, for He said: "You shall worship the Lord your God, and Him only you shall serve" (Matthew 4:10). In quoting this Old Testament passage, Jesus declared the divine priority that worship is first and service is second. This denounced the division of the Church into Marys and Marthas. It is worship *and* service, not worship *or* service. Each of us is to be a worshiper, and out of that worship should flow service.

Christianity and service have always fit together like a hand in a glove, but it is much easier to teach the mechanics of activity than to bring persons into a vital relationship with the Lord Jesus Christ. Many of these active Christians are serving an absentee landlord Who is not only distant, but quite unreal. They have read about Him, and infrequently heard the testimonies of persons who claim to have met Him on some occasion, but the reality of God is unknown to them. Little wonder, then, that their service quickly becomes a job instead of a joy, for dedication wears thin when exhaustion sets in. They need fresh motivation into new endeavors on behalf of this unknown God or their service will completely cease.

This blind service to a deity Who others have defined was characteristic of David's day. King Saul did the minimum service, and that was often done both grudgingly and disobediently. In spite of God's attempts to reach this first king of Israel, Saul remained too self-centered to desire to know Him. When God removed Saul, He chose a replacement who knew his God. David was never a man to be deeply involved in ritual for ritual's sake. Everything he did was as a response to a living God. David knew his God, and he deeply loved the God he knew. God said, "I have found David the son of Jesse, a man after My own heart" (Acts 13:22). Although David was not a perfect man, he loved his God perfectly and served Him faithfully, for he knew Him intimately.

David did not ignore the "historic Christ," as some now call Him, but his excitement was in the living God he had come to know. God was alive to David, and David's responses to God were equally alive. While he never lost sight of the differences between himself and God, he received the grace of God so fully that he responded to God as friend to friend. His wife, Michal, sorely criticized his intimate responses to God, but God loved them. The LORD God had been treated as a distant despot long enough. He was thrilled to have a person on an earthly throne who accepted the divine Presence as real, desirable, and friendly. Since the days of Adam, God had longed for such intimate fellowship with His man, but only on the rarest occasions had He found it. Now He had in David a man who believed that God was, indeed, alive; that He was involved in the here and now, and that He loved His chosen people.

This personal relationship between David and his God is available to all believers. Without it, worship is little more than a religious form or an empty ceremony, but out of this involvement with a personal God will flow a love response that will make worship vital and valid. Today's Church is experiencing an awakening of worship. May she equally enter into a fresh realization that our God is a living God, a present God, and an involved God. Restored relationship with Him must be the first step in worship. Otherwise our worship will be as cold and calloused as the worship of the Pharisees and Sadducees in Jesus' time.

David worshiped a living God. So may we. Perhaps following the footsteps of David as he discovered the nature of this living God will inspire us to "see Him as He is" (1 John 3:2).

CHAPTER 1

David Worshiped a Living God

Overloaded with a huge backpack filled with grain and cheese which were being sent by the father to his seven sons in the army, the undersized lad with red hair and very fair complexion broke over the crest of the hill he had been climbing and looked into the valley below. At first glance, he thought that a prairie fire had swept through the area. Everywhere he looked, he saw large patches of black.

However, this trained keeper of sheep had learned not to trust his first impressions. He eased his pack to the ground and sat down to survey the scene. Before long he could discern movement in and around those black patches, and his ears caught the sound of voices. This was not a burned over area. He was looking at the black goatskin tents of two massed armies facing each other across a narrow valley that separated two hills. This was it! He had found the battlefield. Excitedly, he picked up his pack and started down the hillside toward the camp of Saul's army.

As he got closer to the valley, he discerned a

noticeable difference between the two camps. The camp on his side of the valley seemed somber and silent, while the soldiers in the camp across the valley were boisterous and rowdy. Was it possible that the battle was over, and Israel had lost? Even before he could locate his brothers, the reason for the silence in Israel's camp became clear.

Echoing up from the valley roared the thunderous voice of a heavily armed, nine foot tall giant challenging any soldier in Saul's army to a one-on-one fight to the death. It was to be a substitute for an engagement between the two armies, "winner take all." No amount of rewards offered by King Saul could entice one of his soldiers to respond to such a serious challenge. Stirred almost uncontrollably in his spirit, this lad rushed through Israel's fear-ridden camp seeking his brothers. Quickly unloading his backpack, he asked, "Who is this uncircumcised Philistine, that he should defy the armies of the living God?" (1 Samuel 17:26).

Actually, Goliath had been challenging the armies of King Saul, but this young shepherd had a vastly different concept. As he later explained to the king, his long nights of meditation on God, lying in the meadows and gazing into the heavens as his sheep slept, caused him to try to understand creation. This had led him to believe there was a living God behind it all. Later, when a lion and a bear caught a lamb out of the flock, he found the strength and courage of that living God to kill those devouring beasts. To him, Goliath was no more a challenge than the lion, and the living God was far more interested in protecting His armies than He was in protecting a small flock of sheep.

There is always a contagion in daring, and this absolute conviction of personal knowledge of a living God stirred King Saul to a renewed faith. Although he patiently listened to his military advisors as they pointed out the dangers of allowing this untrained civilian to represent all Israel in this gladiatorial contest, Saul still followed his heart and put the future of Israel in the hands of this brave boy.

Armed with nothing but a slingshot and the Presence of a living God, the boy, despised by his brothers because of his smallness, went out to meet Goliath, loved by the Philistines because of his bigness. Harsh words were exchanged, a challenge was given, a stone was thrown, and Goliath fell mortally wounded. His death brought a colossal victory to the fledgling nation of Israel. When the victor stood holding the severed head of the vanquished challenger, King Saul asked, "Who is this young man?" (see 1 Samuel 17:56).

Who is this young man? Indeed! This is he of whom the women later sang, "Saul has slain his thousands, And David his ten thousands" (1 Samuel 18:7). This youngest son of Jesse, so disdained by his older brothers that they had made him live with the family sheep, was anointed by Samuel to succeed Saul as king. Despised by his family, David became the desire of all Israel.

However, neither the victory over Goliath nor the anointing from Samuel's horn of oil produced an instant ascent to the throne, for God's callings do not become God's commissions until the chosen one has gone through God's college for training. Chosen by God for leadership, David was later chosen by Saul to serve in his court. Then God further conditioned David by forcing him to flee Saul's wrath to spend years in the wilderness amassing a small army of desperados who later became David's "mighty men."

Whether we consider David's achievements as a warrior, a statesman, a politician, a kingdom builder or a worshiper, he had no equal among his peers. To this day, he remains the hero of both Christians and Jews. The song of the women of Israel could be sung in any generation by replacing Saul's name with any name other than God's, and the song would still be valid: "Saul has slain his thousands, and David his tens of thousands." David always excelled.

When Paul said: "David ... served his own generation by the will of God" (Acts 13:36), no Jew in that house of worship would have disputed that statement. How he served his generation! As conqueror, he secured territory as a homeland for his people, and as a statesman, he united the proud tribes of Israel into a functioning and prosperous nation. He was a poet, a musician, a patron of the arts, and he shared with his people his zeal for the release of the cry from a man's soul. David did, indeed, serve his generation, but he equally served the generations that were to follow him, for the territory he conquered became the homeland for the Jews until this day, and the nation that he founded has held together, although it has been dispersed throughout the nations of the world for hundreds of years.

It was in the area of worship that David served both his and our generation so well. David enjoyed worship sessions. He not only participated in them, he demonstrated the release of love and enthusiasm for God in his public worship in eulogy, psalm, song, and dance. To further inspire his people to worship Jehovah, David returned the Ark of the Covenant to Jerusalem. Long viewed as the symbol of God's Presence among His people, the Ark had been unused since its capture by the Philistines during the days of Eli. Neither the prophet Samuel nor King Saul had sought to return it during their reigns, but David felt that the Ark must reside in the capital city — the localized Presence of God must reside among His people.

David pitched a tent for the Ark, for God's first dwelling place among His chosen people had been the elaborate tent known as the Tabernacle in the Wilderness. David's substitute tent was called *The Tabernacle of David,* and this became the focal point of worship; but David longed to build a permanent Temple for the Presence of God. Prohibited by God from doing this because he was responsible for so much bloodshed, God promised David that his son, Solomon, would construct the Temple. Graciously, the LORD gave David the design for the Temple and helped him to amass the materials and wealth needed to build it. He even appointed the craftsmen who would construct the edifice. Before his death, David appointed Solomon as co-regent to assure the nation of a calm transfer of power; and at that time he charged the new king to quickly construct this new house of God.

Even a casual reader of David's life would have to conclude that David was a worshiper! Everything he did was done with an awareness of God. He gave all glory and credit for any accomplishments directly to Jehovah. He seemed to delight in joining the priests and Levites in public display of his exuberant love for God, and his worship was contagious. Who could watch the king worship so unashamedly without joining the celebration?

Much has been said about the uniqueness of David's worship. The heart of the matter is not the different style of David's expression of devotion to God; it is that David consciously worshiped a living God. He wrote, "The LORD lives! Blessed be my Rock! Let the God of my salvation be exalted" (Psalm 18:46). It was this concept that made David's worship so outstanding in his generation and the many generations that have followed him. His responses, whether in word, song, or behavior, were responses to a Person Who was as much alive to David as Joab, the general of his armies.

Although David loved the Law of God, he did not restrict his worship responses to quoting that Law. The Psalms reveal that David cried from the depths of his inner spirit, and he talked to God about things natural as well as things spiritual. He expressed his positive and negative emotions to God in his seasons of worship. In David's mind, God was alive and concerned about him.

David did not devise this concept of a living God. The patriarchs had known an existing God, and they had sought to pass that reality on to others. But years of religious ritual had concealed this truth from most people. Samuel had discovered it, but he was an unusual person for his generation. While we cannot credit David with discovering this truth, we can credit him for rediscovering it, and we must admit that he delighted in it.

It was this concept that Jehovah was a living God that became the underlying force of David's life. It was the source of his courage against the giant, Goliath. It was the heart of his bravery in warfare, for he wrote: "Blessed be the LORD my Rock, Who trains my hands for war, And my fingers for battle ... My high tower and my deliverer, My shield and the One in whom I take refuge, Who subdues my people under me" (Psalm 144:1-2). This king actually believed that the battles he fought were the wars of God, and the living God would strengthen him for conflict and protect him during the battle. David knew much opposition, both from enemies without and friends within, yet he wrote, "In the day when I cried out, You answered me, And made me bold with strength in my soul" (Psalm 138:3). David consistently saw God as the balancing side of every equation in life. With God beside him, he considered himself invincible. Little wonder, then, that David became an overcomer in all things — even his gross errors and his obnoxious sins.

David Worshiped a Living God in Contrast to Idolatry

David's concept of a living God is all the more remarkable when we realize that the surrounding nations were completely idolatrous. Even the very people he served were not totally free from idolatry. While others served a god of cast metal, David worshiped a God Whose image was mental. He did not have a carved image of stone to give form to his concept of God. David had the Law of God carved into stone by the very finger of God!

David was far less concerned with the image of God than he was with the Person of God. In one of the Songs of Ascents, many of which are credited to him, we read David's view of idols: "The idols of the nations are silver and gold, The work of men's hands. They have mouths, but they do not speak: Eyes they have, but they do not see; They have ears, but they do not hear; Nor is there any breath in their mouths. Those who make them are like them; so is everyone who trusts in them." In contrast to this, he cries, "Bless the LORD, O house of Israel! Bless the LORD, O house of Aaron! Bless the LORD, O house of Levi! You who fear the LORD, bless the LORD! Blessed be the LORD out of Zion, Who dwells in Jerusalem! Praise the LORD!" (Psalm 135:15-21).

David came into the scene of world history when the belief in many gods — polytheism — was universally embraced. The surrounding nations served a great variety of gods, and they had an empirical structure of lesser gods and greater gods. From the day that Jehovah had appeared to Abraham, through all of His dealings with the family of Israel, God had declared Himself to be a divine monopoly, and He demanded that His people worship no other God than Himself. David strictly adhered to this, and was completely mono-theistic in belief and practice. To him, Jehovah was not merely a god, He was the true and living God. Beside Him, there was none other. For this reason, the idol gods of the nations around him created no fear in David. He viewed them as figments of men's imagin-ations. He was convinced they were powerless to prevent him from doing what the living God had instructed him to do.

Looking backwards, his position seems logical, but David did not stand with the majority. Jehovah was often viewed as an absentee Landlord to whom rent had to be paid, or He was visualized as a harsh, exacting Being who had to be propitiated constantly through sacrifice and service. David insisted that Jehovah was a loving God, present among His people and deeply concerned in all matters of their welfare. When David offered sacrifices, it was far less for propitiation than it was for praise. He did not see himself as much as a worker for God, but as a worshiper of God. He didn't even divide his life into the sacred and the secular; he and his God lived together in all aspects of life. This was totally inconsistent with idolatry, but it was consistent with the revelation of God that David had received.

David Worshiped a Living God in Contrast to Ritual

Any person who would argue against ritual in the worship of God must argue with God Himself, for He established a most elaborate worship ritual when He gave Moses the plans for the Tabernacle in the Wilder-ness and the manner in which the priests were to bring the worship of the people before Himself. There were specific garments for certain functions and very precise methods of offering the different sacrifices. There were days for fasting and days for feasting. There were voluntary holy days and there were compulsory convocations. So involved and elaborate was this system of rituals that Levite priests began training for service at least five years before being consecrated to the priesthood.

The purpose of ritual may be multitudinous. As long as it helps persons in their worship it can be valuable, but the danger lies in it becoming a substitute for worship instead of a channel for that adoration. Back in 1524, Thomas Bilney, a Fellow of Trinity Hall in whose heart was born the Reformation at Cambridge University, said to Hugh Latimer, a priest of Cambridge who became the Bishop of Worcester and the King's preacher: "Aids to worship have turned into obstacles to keep us from reaching God at all. Ceremonies intended to help us show our devotion to Christ have become means of winning His love and forgiveness, even of earning salvation. His lovely face is obscured by the wrong use of ceremonial aids." (LATIMER, Apostle to the English, by Sarah H. Stuart; page 25, Zondervan Publishing House, Grand Rapids, MI. c.1986.)

Just how forceful ritual was in the days of David is difficult to tell. The Tabernacle of the Wilderness had already fallen into ruin. Only the Ark of the Covenant survived, and this was not responded to during the entire lifetime and ministry of Samuel and King Saul. The principle of oblation was maintained; Samuel, and occasionally even Saul, offered sacrifices to Jehovah even though the Aaronic priesthood, as established by God, had virtually disappeared at the death of Eli and his sons. Samuel functioned as both prophet and priest, with the near authority of a king, until the people chose Saul to rule over them. But this loss of the elaborate did not diminish the dependence of the people upon the ritual, for the only continuity of worship left was the remembered rituals that Moses had handed down, especially the blood sacrifices. These they continued to offer in a variety of places under the headship of the father of the family, who acted as the priest for his home.

Separated from a priesthood, a specific place of worship and the Law of God, except as proclaimed by the occasional prophet in the land, the worship of Israel in those days lacked a personal involvement with God. The emphasis was upon the act of worship (sacrifice) rather than the One worshiped. David had experienced a relationship with the True and Living God, and his worship reflected this. On the hills of Bethlehem, David had learned to worship God without ritual. When he became king, he sought to bring his subjects into worship that was a response to a Living Being as well as a release of inner love for God.

Since he had found such release toward God in singing, David introduced the use of music in the worship of Jehovah. He wrote over half of the Psalms in the hymnbook of the Bible, and many of them are specifically dedicated to public worship. David invented several musical instruments and manufactured them for use by the Levites in their worship of Jehovah. He reinstituted the Levitical priesthood and arranged several hundred of them into a musical division, forming choirs and orchestras. He divided these into twenty-four units so both instrumental and choral music could be played around the clock before the returned Ark of the Covenant in Jerusalem.

While David embraced the ritual of sacrifice, he also

enlarged the worship experience with rejoicing in song and dance. He revived the communal feasts of the Lord and at least three times a year gathered the people together in Jerusalem to celebrate God. Since our response in worship will be consistent with our concept of God, David's perception of a living God strongly influenced his manner of response to God. He, in turn, changed the way the people worshiped Jehovah. He put reality into their ritual by teaching his people that worship was a deliberate and loving response to a living God.

David Worshiped a Living God in Contrast to a Historic One

Perhaps nothing can destroy the reality of worship faster than locking it into a historical concept of God. While the God of yesterday can set the pattern for our concept of the God of today, God is far more than the deity of our fathers or of children yet to be born. "Jesus Christ is the same yesterday, today, and forever" (Hebrews 13:8). God is the God of NOW, not merely the God of then. David had a firm grasp on this concept. Seldom do his Psalms speak of the God of Abraham, Isaac, and Jacob; he consistently speaks of "MY God." He revealed his concept of God when he wrote: "God is our refuge and strength, A very present help in trouble" (Psalm 46:1). The literal Hebrew for "present help" is "an abundantly available help." David never had to reach for the God of Moses for help; he reached for David's God. "The LORD of hosts is with us," he cried (Psalm 46:7).

It was this awareness of a God of the NOW that affected David's prayers. He communicated with God as a present Person, and he expected a response. He

petitioned a reigning Monarch, and he assumed intervention. While David may have projected qualities and
characteristics to God that are totally human, it does
indicate the oneness that he felt with God. If David was
disgusted with impropriety, he assumed that God was
equally indignant over the injustice. When David was
angry, he assumed that God was proportionally angry,
and when David felt that he should intervene in any
given situation, he presumed that God would intervene
with him. Somehow David had entered into a partner-
ship with God that caused him to cry, "Our God shall
come, and shall not keep silent" (Psalm 50:3). David's
God was never inactive; He was always a functioning
partner. To him, prayer was always communication
with a living, caring Person. Although David often
reached into history in his Psalms, he loved to bring
them into the present tense when speaking of God.
"One generation shall praise Your works to another,
And shall declare Your mighty acts," he wrote; then he
added: "The LORD is gracious and full of compassion ...
The LORD is good to all, And His tender mercies are
over all His works" (Psalm 145:4,8-9). David moved
from historic concepts of God to present attitudes
without hesitation. He fully credited God with the
great deliverances of His people in generations past,
but David was locked into a concept of a living, present
God Whose unchangeableness made Him as available
to David as He had been to Moses or Joshua. "The
LORD is near to all who call upon Him" (Psalm 145:18)
seemed to be David's theme. This made his praise and
worship very vital and personal. He knew the God he
was worshiping. David did not need to praise God
merely for deeds in the past, for He was involved in
divine works in the immediate present, and this was
the occasion for most of his praise.

Because David's God was far more a contemporary companion than a historic hero, David told his generation, "The LORD of hosts is with us; The God of Jacob is our refuge" (Psalm 46:7). He challenged them to "Commit your way to the LORD, Trust also in Him, And He shall bring it to pass ... Rest in the LORD, and wait patiently for Him ... The steps of a good man are ordered by the LORD, And He delights in his way ... The salvation of the righteous is from the LORD; He is their strength in the time of trouble. And the LORD shall help them and deliver them; He shall deliver them from the wicked, And save them, Because they trust in him" (Psalm 37:5,7,23,39-40).

David could never conceive his relationship with God as being short-term. Since Jehovah was as real in David's present as He would ever be in the future, David believed that his association with the Almighty not only touched all measurements of time, but extended into timeless eternity. Although he lived many hundreds of years before Jesus proclaimed, "Because I live, you shall live also" (John 14:19), David possessed the hope that the living God he served would share that life with him throughout all eternity. He was content to let the scribes of his day wrestle with the God of Abraham and Moses; David related to the living God of his generation. He sang, "You will show me the path of life; In Your Presence is fullness of joy; At Your right hand are pleasures forevermore" (Psalm 16:11).

David Worshiped a Living God in Contrast to His Contemporaries

Three times Asaph, David's musical understudy, cried: "Why should the heathen say, 'Where is their God?' " (Psalm 42:3,10; 79:10), and this same question is posed by an unnamed psalmist in Psalm 115:2. Quite obviously, then, David's contemporaries were quite aware of the constant challenge of the heathen idolaters of the surrounding countries: "Show us your God!" They had elaborate temples to house their stone and metal gods, but David had pitched only a tent to house the Ark of the Covenant. They often carried their carved images into battle, but David never allowed the Ark to leave Jerusalem.

Perhaps this seems inconsequential to us, but we need to remember how small a minority David's Israel was in comparison to the many nations that surrounded his tiny territory. David consistently led small troops against a larger army, and often several kings joined forces in trying to overthrow him. When they made such an open display of the presence of their gods and cried taunting jeers at Israel asking them to display their God, David had to have an answer for his men. In describing this situation, David wrote, "At evening they return, They growl like a dog, And go all around the city. Indeed, they belch with their mouth; Swords are in their lips; For they say, 'Who hears?' But You, O LORD, shall laugh at them; You shall have all the nations in derision. I will wait for You, O You his Strength. For God is my defense. My God of mercy shall come to meet me; God shall let me see my desire on my enemies" (Psalm 59:6-10).

David revealed God in function rather than in form. He did not feel the need for an idol representation of Jehovah, nor did he feel that carrying the Ark into battle was proper. His God was a living God, and David was convinced that His divine Presence was demonstrated by His performance. David admitted that his dependence was totally in this real Presence, for he wrote: " 'If it had not been the LORD who was on our side,' Let Israel now say — 'If it had not been the LORD

Who was on our side, When men rose up against us, Then they would have swallowed us alive, When their wrath was kindled against us' ... Blessed be the LORD, Who has not given us as prey to their teeth. Our soul has escaped as a bird from the snare of the fowlers; The snare is broken, and we have escaped. Our help is in the name of the LORD" (Psalm 124:1-3,6-8).

Idol worshipers could not conceive of worshiping their gods any place other than in their temples or before the idol images, and even most Hebrews of David's day limited their worship responses to feast days when they had the services of the Levitical priesthood. Not David! Although he reveled in the feasts of the Lord, he worshiped God anywhere and everywhere, because he was conscious of an ever-present, living God. He could sing, "When I remember You on my bed, I meditate on You in the night watches. Because You have been my help, Therefore in the shadow of Your wings I will rejoice. My soul follows close behind You; Your right hand upholds me" (Psalm 63:6-8). Furthermore, he affirmed, "I will bless the LORD at all times; His praise shall continually be in my mouth" (Psalm 34:1). David let the prophets depend upon their musicians, and he let the priests lean upon their ritual. He worshiped God in his home, on the throne, on the battlefield, and especially in the tent he had pitched for the Ark of the Covenant. That is the advantage of serving a living God. He is always present. David poetically declared this when he sang, "Where can I go from Your Spirit? Or where can I flee from Your Presence? If I ascend into heaven, You are there; If I make my bed in hell, behold, you are there. If I take the wings of the morning, And dwell in the uttermost parts of the sea, Even there Your hand shall lead me, And Your right hand shall hold me. If I say, 'Surely the darkness shall fall on me,' Even the night shall be light about me; Indeed, the darkness shall not hide from you" (Psalm 139:7-12). What a precious and practical concept of God this illustrious king possessed!

David Worshiped a Living God in Contrast to His Successors

David's concept was neither new nor novel, but it was out of step with his peers, and it remained out of step for the kings who followed him upon the throne. Solomon, David's son, built the Temple to Jehovah, but he also built temples to idol gods to please some of the many wives he married. Unfortunately, they eventually turned his heart from serving the true and living God to joining them in their worship of idols. By the time David's grandson was on the throne, there seemed to be no concept of a living God. Ritual replaced reality and form replaced a functioning God. Idolatry was soon rampant throughout the divided land.

David was neither the first nor the last parent who did not pass his faith in a living God to his progeny. Testimonies of God's interventions can be passed on, and concepts of God's nature may be taught, but only a personal encounter and subsequent experience with the living God can instill the abiding faith that characterized David's life. Even a casual reading of the prophets whom God raised up in the generations subsequent to David's will convince us that few persons entered into this experiential relationship with God.

The route from David, where God was the ever-present living God, to the days of Daniel, where God was seen as the absentee Warden over His captive people exiled in Babylon, was progressive. First, Israel formalized their worship in Solomon's elaborate Temple. Next, they limited their worship to the feast days, then sought to make their worship more convenient by burning incense on various hills around their villages. This led to the abandonment of the Temple; a turning from directing their worship to Jehovah to worshiping the various Baals; and finally, they openly embraced idols in full replacement of Jehovah. For this, God sold them into slavery.

Departure from a vital relationship with God is always progressive, and it frequently follows a similar route. When worship by identification replaces participation in worship, we have already entered the road of departure. It will not be long until we desire a more convenient way to worship, which quickly leads to a substitute object of worship. Once God has been replaced as the focal point of our worship, almost any image that seems religious will satisfy us, and our idolatry will cause God to sell us into captivity.

The Bible honestly records several of David's sins and failures to prevent us from idolizing a man that God loved; but for all the delinquency of David's flesh, he never forsook the worship of a true and living God during his lifetime. In the last days of his life, after he had anointed Solomon, his son, to be king in his place, "David blessed the LORD before all the assembly; and David said: 'Blessed are You, LORD God of Israel, our Father, forever and ever. Yours, O LORD, is the greatness, The power and the glory, The victory and the majesty; For all that is in the heaven and in earth is Yours; Yours is the kingdom, O Lord. And You are exalted as head over all' " (1 Chronicles 29:10-11).

David's concept of the living God accelerated rather than diminished all the days of his life, for he sought to know the God that he loved and worshiped. One of the ways David came to know God was through the revelation that comes in the very names of God, for

God is a self-revealing God Who desires that His children mature in their knowledge of Him. This knowledge comes by divine *declaration,* as in the Law; by divine *demonstration,* as in God's miraculous interventions; and by divine *designation,* as in the names God has given to Himself. David loved all three forms of revelation. It may very well have been David who wrote: "Oh, how I love Your law! It is my meditation all the day ... Your testimonies are my meditation. I understand more than the ancients, Because I keep Your precepts" (Psalm 119:97,99-100).

That David had learned about God from His marvelous deeds is clear. He wrote: "We have heard with our ears, O God, Our fathers have told us the deeds You did in their days, In days of old: You drove out the nations with Your hand, But them You planted ... It was Your right hand, Your arm, and the light of Your countenance, Because You favored them. You are my King, O God; Command victories for Jacob. Through You we will push down our enemies; Through Your name we will trample those who rise up against us" (Psalm 44:1-5). David saw God's historic handiwork and dared to trust that the everlasting LORD would do in the present what He had done in the past.

As surely as David learned experientially about God through divine declarations and demonstrations, David also learned about God through the declaration of His name. He sang: "According to Your name, O God, So is Your praise to the ends of the earth" (Psalm 48:10). This progressive revelation of God that came to David through the compound names of Jehovah affected his worship of God for the rest of his life. May that same revelation affect our worship responses in the days that yet remain for us, as David's revelation affected his son

Solomon, who wrote: "The name of the LORD is a strong tower; The righteous run to it and are safe" (Proverbs 18:10).

CHAPTER 2

David Knew
the God He Worshiped

Men who have achieved greatness in the kingdom of God have all asked one question of God: "Who are You?" Saul, who later became the apostle Paul, while traveling on the road to Damascus was smitten to the ground by the brightness of God's Presence and cried out, "Who are You, Lord?" (Acts 9:5). Saul needed to know with Whom he was dealing before he knew how to respond. Paul, theologically trained in the school of Gamaliel, couldn't fit this experience into his theology. He was about to embark upon a lifetime training course in knowing God, and God Himself was to be his teacher.

Moses experienced a similar frustration after he intervened in Israel's worship of the Golden Calf. Having seen the righteous judgments of God, and having participated in God's vengeance, Moses cried out, "Please, show me Your glory" (Exodus 33:18). Moses felt that he had come to the place where he could no longer lead Israel until he knew God better. The knowledge of God that he had gained at the burning bush did not cover what he was experiencing from God.

God instructed him to return to the mountain and stand in a chosen place where a large rock was split, and "The Lord passed before him and proclaimed, 'The LORD, the LORD God, merciful and gracious, long-suffering, and abounding in goodness and truth, keeping mercy for thousands, forgiving iniquity and transgression and sin, by no means clearing the guilty, visiting the iniquity of the fathers upon the children and the children's children to the third and the fourth generation'" (Exodus 34:6-7). This, as expected, evoked an immediate worship response from Moses, for "Moses made haste and bowed his head toward the earth, and worshiped" (Exodus 34:8).

These two outstanding men of God — Moses, representing the Old Testament, and Paul, a key New Testament figure — understood that it is God's will that we know Him. They recognized their need for an unfolding revelation of God and God's need to give that self-revelation. Over 76 times, the Old Testament says, "... know that I am the LORD." God has never issued a command without also providing an ability to fulfill that command. If God says that we should know Him, then the responsibility for that revelation of God rests with God Himself. Our responsibility is to be good students.

David, whose writings stand between Moses and Paul, also cried out to know God. In one of his early Psalms, he wrote, "Show me Your ways, O LORD: Teach me Your paths. Lead me in Your truth and teach me, For You are the God of my salvation; On You I wait all the day." Then he expressed his confidence, "The

secret of the LORD is with those who fear Him, And He
will show them His covenant'' (Psalm 25:4-5,14).
Another time he sang, "All my bones shall say, 'LORD,
who is like You?' '' (Psalm 35:10). On yet another
occasion he exclaimed, "One thing I have desired of the
LORD, That will I seek: That I may dwell in the house
of the LORD all the days of my life, To behold the
beauty of the LORD, And to inquire in His temple''
(Psalm 27:4). There can be no question that David was
joining Moses and Paul in their quest to know the God
they served.

David's Knowledge of God Came from SCRIPTURE

If David ever had a personal meeting with God such
as Moses had on the mountain, or Paul had on the road
to Damascus, the Bible does not mention it. It is always
dangerous to expect God to do things the same way for
different people, for God is a God of infinite variety,
Who chooses His own means of self-revelation. While
David, of course, had no knowledge of what would later
happen to Saul of Tarsus, he probably did have access
to the story of what happened to Moses.

In the days before printing made the Scriptures
widely available, oral tradition, songs, odes, and poems
passed on much truth from one generation to another.
David referred to this when he sang, "One generation
shall praise Your works to another'' (Psalm 145:4).
David came from a godly tribe, Judah, and he was a
resident of Bethlehem, which would later become the
birthplace of Jesus. We have every reason to believe
that he received much teaching about God in his youth.
Furthermore, as king over all Israel, he probably had
access to the Law of Moses. In speaking of the righteous,
he said, "The law of his God is in his heart'' (Psalm
37:31), and David was certainly a righteous person.

Although the first Psalm does not carry David's name in its inscription, it is in the collection of David's Psalms. Many people credit it to this godly king. In it we read, "Blessed is the man who walks not in the counsel of the ungodly ... But his delight is in the law of the LORD, And in His law he meditates day and night" (Psalm 1:1-2).

David's Psalms give repeated evidence of his comprehensive knowledge of God's Law, but, perhaps more than any person since Moses, David came to know the God of the Law even better than he knew the Law of God. David repeated the seven aspects of the divine nature that God declared to Moses again and again throughout the Psalter. God had revealed Himself to Moses as (1) merciful, (2) gracious, (3) longsuffering, (4) abounding in goodness, (5) abounding in truth, (6) abounding in mercy, (7) forgiving iniquity, transgression and sin. David embraced this revelation, and he read the Law through the filter of this divine disclosure. Accordingly, he could grasp the nature of God in His Law rather than merely seeing the judicial requirements of God's Law.

God had said that He was *merciful.* That settled it for David; he wrote, "With the merciful You will show Yourself merciful," and "Also to You, O LORD, belongs mercy; For You render to each one according to his work" (Psalms 18:25; 62:12). David felt that God would respond to like nature. God had also declared Himself to be *gracious, longsuffering,* abounding in *truth* and *mercy,* and David wrote: "But You, O LORD, are a God full of compassion, and gracious, longsuffering and abundant in mercy and truth" (Psalm 86:15). David demonstrated that he understood God's statement that He abounded in *goodness* by his repeated statement, "The LORD is good ... " He invited others, "Oh, taste and see that the LORD is good; Blessed is the man who trusts in Him!'' (Psalm 34:8). He shouted throughout the Psalter about the *forgiving* nature of God. "For You, LORD, are good, and ready to forgive, And abundant in mercy to all those who call upon You,'' he wrote (Psalm 86:5). He also contemplated, "Blessed is he whose transgression is forgiven, Whose sin is covered. Blessed is the man to whom the LORD does not impute iniquity ... I acknowledged my sin to You, And my iniquity I have not hidden. I said, 'I will confess my transgressions to the LORD,' And you forgave the iniquity of my sin'' (Psalm 32:1-2,5).

To David, the divine Law was an expression of the divine nature of God, and David appropriated that nature into the affairs of his life. He was not dependent upon principles, for he had met the Person Who gave the Law, and since he knew the God he worshiped, he embraced the principles of His Law as revelations of His divine nature.

David's Knowledge of God Came from PROGRESSIVE REVELATION

As some persons learn history while others learn from history, David was one who could learn about God from His dealings in the lives of others. Many persons see only the performance of God in the lives of others. David seemed to see a pattern and could discover a principle of the nature of God in what was happening. This enabled him to apply that principle to his own life and circumstances. He did not have to rediscover God. He could enter into what others had discovered about God and use this as a platform from which he launched his own search after God.

David's Psalms also show a thorough knowledge of Israel's history and of God's dealings with His people.

Whether Nathan, the prophet, helped David to see beyond the historic actions of God into the divine nature of God, or whether this was the direct work of the Holy Spirit within this chosen vessel is unknown to us. What is known is that David had an uncanny ability to see the nature of God revealed in the actions of God. When David rehearsed the story of Israel crossing through the Red Sea, he saw beyond the miracle and grasped the motive for God's action. Later, he could apply this concept of God in his own life. Substituting the image of fire for that of water, he wrote, "Your hand will find all Your enemies; Your right hand will find those who hate You. You shall make them as a fiery oven in the time of Your anger; The LORD shall swallow them up in His wrath, And the fire shall devour them. Their offspring You shall destroy from the earth, And their descendants from among the sons of men. For they intended evil against You; They devised a plot which they are not able to perform" (Psalm 21:8-11).

In saying, "Some trust in chariots, and some in horses; but we will remember the name of the LORD our God. They have bowed down and fallen; But we have risen and stand upright" (Psalm 20:7-8), David likely alluded to the crossing of the Red Sea, but he makes a present tense application. Similarly, in referring to the flood in Noah's day, he wrote, "The LORD sat enthroned at the Flood, And the LORD sits as King forever" (Psalm 29:10). In saying that God "Made known His ways to Moses, His acts to the children of Israel" (Psalm 103:7), David saw beyond this fact to the character of God and added, "The LORD is merciful and gracious, slow to anger, and abounding in mercy" (verse 8). Again and again, David saw beyond God's behavior to behold God.

David was so aware of God's unchanging nature that whatever revelation He had given of Himself to others, he quickly embraced as his own. He then reached for additional personal revelation. He accepted the self-revelation God had given to Abraham, Moses, Joshua and others, but repeatedly, he expressed that same concept at a higher level. Progressive revelation works that way, both in the natural realm and the spiritual realm. One scientific breakthrough opens the path for many more breakthroughs. Spiritually, every concept of God that becomes practical forms a platform for greater understanding of the nature of God. Having listed several consecutive things that He would do for Judah, God said, " 'Then I will give them a heart to know Me, that I am the LORD; and they shall be My people, and I will be their God, for they shall return to Me with their whole heart' " (Jeremiah 24:7). This knowledge of God was to be progressive, and it required a performance to unfold the very Person of God. Furthermore, it was dependent upon God's gift of an understanding heart — "Then I will give them a heart to know Me ..." It is obvious that God gave such a heart to David.

David's Knowledge of God Came from PERSONAL EXPERIENCES

While the authority of God's Word does not rest in our experiences, embracing the revelation of God's Word, both written and Living [Christ Jesus], brings us into spiritual experiences that can be life-transforming. These experiences do not become the basis of faith, but they do become powerful expressions of our faith, and an analytical viewer will find those experiences great instructors of faith. Repeatedly, the Bible records personal encounters with God that were life-changing to individuals. The divine intervention made a dramatic difference.

Far from being the exception, David was exemplary of this fact. From the day that Samuel called him from tending sheep to anoint him to be king over Israel, David had experience after experience that changed his behavior and formed his concepts of God. God's choice of David to be leader of Israel convinced David of God's sovereignty. He, or another psalmist, recorded, "Our God is in heaven; He does whatever He pleases" (Psalm 115:3). Similarly, David's great victory over Goliath forever imprinted upon David's conscious mind the extraordinary power of God available to His covenant people. Years later, he wrote: "God has spoken once, Twice I have heard this: That power belongs to God" (Psalm 62:11).

The difficult years that David spent in training under the king that God had rejected taught this king-in-waiting much about the longsuffering of God. He watched God put up with Saul's rebellion, pride, self-seeking and jealousy just because he was God's anointed for the office. This so impressed David that he would not touch God's anointed. Having seen God to be long-suffering, David felt that he, too, could suffer long with Saul. Experience may be a painful teacher, but her lessons are long remembered.

The lengthy season that David hid from the wrath of King Saul unveiled God's great protective power so forcefully that in Psalm after Psalm, David speaks of God under the simile of military protection, calling Him his high tower, his shield, his hiding place, his fortress, etc. He declared, "My defense is of God, Who saves the upright in heart" (Psalm 7:10). This is one aspect of the nature of God that David had to lean on repeatedly during his lifetime.

When God sensed that David was ready for leadership, He allowed Saul to be killed in warfare. Following this, He installed David as king over Judah for seven years and later united the entire kingdom under David's leadership. David never forgot how God faithfully keeps His word. He came to know that if God said it, He will perform it. When the Ark was returned to Jerusalem, David sang, "He remembers His covenant forever, The word which He commanded, for a thousand generations" (Psalm 105:8). David learned this long before he sang it.

David's lustful involvement with Bathsheba escalated into the murder of her husband, Uriah. The aftermath of this taught David principles of God's mercy and forgiveness that he never forgot. He later testified: "For You, Lord, are good, and ready to forgive, And abundant in mercy to all those who call upon You" (Psalm 86:5).

Again and again, David had life experiences in which he saw the hand of God intervening on his behalf. Through these, he came to know the living God in a most intimate way. Personal experience is a valid teaching tool in the ways of God.

However, it is not *what* happens to us as much as *how* we respond to those happenings that make experience such a forceful teaching tool. The historic account of the life of David could be read without actually seeing the hand of God involved, for God used natural means and human instrumentality to accomplish His ends. Accordingly, David could have lived his life without seeing God's involvement in it. He could have credited the slaying of Goliath to his skill with a sling, and he might have accepted his choice for kingship as a matter of chance. But David had come to know God, and from that point on, everything spoke of Jehovah to

David. He had learned to expect the participation of God in his day-to-day experiences, and his expectations were not in vain.

The Bible does not give a complete history of any person. When David first met God is not known, but it is likely that it happened during his youth while he was tending his father's sheep, for when he was chosen for kingship he showed no surprise. He acted as though he had known it all the time and was relieved to have his family know it. It is likely that God had communicated this to David directly, and then used Samuel to confirm it and make it known to the public. David's shepherd Psalm (Psalm 23) further shows that the young shepherd had begun to know the living God and was embracing Him as "MY Shepherd."

David's Knowledge of God Came from INTIMATE RELATIONSHIP

That there is a God in heaven is not as dramatic a revelation as that this great God *knows me*. David was amazed at this truth, for he wrote: "But You are He who took Me out of the womb; You made Me trust while on My mother's breasts. I was cast upon You from birth. From My mother's womb You have been My God" (Psalm 22:9-10). He also asked, "LORD, what is man, that You take knowledge of him? Or the son of man, that You are mindful of him?" (Psalm 144:3). This intimate knowledge that God possessed about David's life was so overwhelming to him that he wrote, "O LORD, You have searched me and known me. You know my sitting down and my rising up; You understand my thought afar off, You comprehend my path and my lying down, And are acquainted with all my ways. For there is not a word on my tongue, But behold, O LORD, You know it altogether. You have hedged me behind and before, And laid Your hand upon me. Such knowledge is too wonderful for me; It is high, I cannot attain it'' (Psalm 139:1-6).

David did not seem to be overwhelmed with his comprehension of the existence of God, for he assumed that the evidence was so irrefutable that everyone could grasp it. He wrote, "The heavens declare the glory of God; And the firmament shows His handiwork. Day unto day utters speech, And night unto night reveals knowledge. There is no speech nor language where their voice is not heard. Their line has gone out through all the earth, And their words to the end of the world'' (Psalm 19:1-4). God in heaven is one matter, but God in the heart is entirely different. It was the awareness that this great Creator knew David intimately that made God so alive to him. He wrote, "But I am poor and needy; Yet the LORD thinks upon me" (Psalm 40:17). Out of this awareness David drew confidence in God. He wrote, "God is our refuge and strength, A very present help in trouble" (Psalm 46:1).

David's greatness was totally the work of God. Through the prophet Nathan, God told David, "Thus says the LORD of hosts: 'I took you from the sheepfold, from following the sheep, to be ruler over My people, over Israel. And I have been with you wherever you have gone, and have cut off all your enemies from before you, and have made you a great name, like the name of the great men who are on the earth' " (2 Samuel 7:8-9). David wrote a Psalm that recounts many of his victories and accomplishments, but through it all he gives the ultimate credit to God. He said, "Your gentleness has made me great ... You enlarged my path under me ... You have armed me with strength for the battle ... You have given me the necks of my enemies ... You have made me the head of the nations." To this he added, "The LORD lives! Blessed be my Rock! Let the God of my salvation be exalted" (Psalm 18:35,36,39 40,43,46).

Throughout the Bible, it has been this awareness that Almighty God actually knows individuals here on this earth that has made the reality of God so vivid. At the burning bush, Moses was amazed that the bush was not consumed in the fire, but this miraculous event deteriorated when compared with God's calling Moses by his name. What had started as a phenomenon became a personal experience with God the moment God called Moses by his name. God knew him individually, and Moses aspired to know God personally.

Saul's experience was similar. This zealous Pharisee dedicated himself to protecting the purity and holiness of God no matter how many persons of "The Way" he had to imprison or slaughter. His conversion experience began with a voice from heaven saying, "Saul, Saul, why are you persecuting Me?" (Acts 26:14). The message took on a depth of meaning because God convinced Saul that He was both living and involved in the affairs of the day, simply by calling Saul by his name.

Again and again, God used this tactic throughout the Bible. He knows how difficult it is for us to respond to an abstract idea or event or to rally to a good cause, so He reveals Himself as a Person who actually knows us. Through the prophet God declared, "But now, thus says the LORD, who created you, O Jacob, And He who formed you, O Israel: 'Fear not, for I have redeemed you; I have called you by your name; You are Mine. When you pass through the waters, I will be with you; And through the rivers, they shall not overflow you. When you walk through the fire, you shall not be burned, Nor shall the flame scorch you. For I am the

LORD your God, The Holy One of Israel, your Savior' "
(Isaiah 43:1-3).

It is always an astounding revelation to discover that
our Creator, our Redeemer, our Protector, and the
Holy One knows us so individually that He calls us by
name and promises to walk with us through life's
experiences. It is greater than our ability to call every
ant in an anthill by name, or being able to identify
individual bees in a hive. We certainly would not offer
to be involved in the affairs of every tiny ant or flying
bee as God has offered to be involved with us.

We habitually view humanity as an immense mass
of people, but God relates to us as individuals. He
recognizes the differences among us, and He makes no
attempt to catalog or classify us. His greatness can
accommodate our smallness, and in His omniscience
every detail of our lives is ever before Him. Still, He
loves us! Because of that love, He has pledged Himself
to be with us in everything we encounter in life. The
three Hebrew children had nothing over us. The same
God that walked with them in the flaming furnace has
pledged to walk with us through our panicky present
and our fearful future. He knows us as surely as He
knew them.

Many years ago, the national leader of the denom-
ination in which I was serving the Lord was the
speaker at a state-wide convention of ministers and
delegates. I honored and respected him for his leadership, but I did not know him as a person. You can
imagine my surprise when, at the end of his message,
he leaned across the pulpit and called me by name,
asking me to go to the organ to assist him with the altar
call. I had no idea that he knew me personally. I had
never been introduced to him, yet he had taken the
time to gather information about me. He later shared

with me how fully he knew me and the work I was doing. From that day on, my relationship with him was entirely different. It became personal rather than organizational.

So it is with our relationship with God. As long as we merely know about Him, we will be distant in our relationship, but when we discover that He actually knows us intimately, we respond personally. Worship will always remain cold and ritualistic until we realize that God is a living God Who knows and loves us individually. It was this awareness of a living God that made David's worship so vibrant and enduring, and it will take that same personal relationship to lift our worship from the realms of mere religion into the realms of the divine.

David enhanced his conviction that God lived by this personal relationship he enjoyed with God. God's intimate knowledge of David and His personal concern for His people combined in David to produce a most practical relationship that placed God as a working partner in all of David's affairs. David did not merely call upon God in emergencies; he called upon God regularly. He wrote: "I remember You on my bed, I meditate on You in the night watches. Because You have been my help, Therefore in the shadow of Your wings I will rejoice. My soul follows close behind You; Your right hand upholds me" (Psalm 63:6-8). Since David knew the God he worshiped, his worship was relational, repetitive, and real. This is reflected throughout the Psalms by David's use of "the LORD *is*; the LORD *Who*; the LORD *my*; the LORD ... *you/your*."

David's Knowledge of God Came from God's SELF-REVELATION

The Bible pointedly teaches that God wants us to

know Him, not merely know about Him. The fundamental purpose of the Bible is to reveal a living God to a
dying race. The stated purpose for the incarnation was
to reveal God to mankind. The angel told Joseph,
" 'Behold, the virgin shall be with child, and bear a Son,
and they shall call His name Immanuel, which is
translated, "God with us." ' " (Matthew 1:23), and in
His High Priestly prayer, Jesus told the Father, " 'And
this is eternal life, that they may know You, the only
true God, and Jesus Christ whom You have sent' "
(John 17:3).

The incarnation succeeded in revealing God to us. As
one who lived and ministered with Jesus, John testified:
"And we know that the Son of God has come and has
given us an understanding, that we may know Him
who is true; and we are in Him who is true, in His Son
Jesus Christ. This is the true God and eternal life" (1
John 5:20). Because this knowledge of God is available,
Paul dared to cry, "That I may know Him and the
power of His resurrection, and the fellowship of His
sufferings, being conformed to His death ... " (Philippians 3:10).

Paul yearned to know God intimately just a short
season after the death of Jesus, but the psalmist
expressed a similar cry many hundreds of years before
Christ's birth. He wrote: "That they may know that
You, whose name alone is the LORD, Are the Most
High over all the earth" (Psalm 83:18). David expressed
this desire in somewhat different terms when he
wrote: "Show me Your ways, O LORD; teach me Your
paths. Lead me in Your truth and teach me, For You
are the God of my salvation; On You I wait all the day"
(Psalm 25:4-5).

There is a God-shaped vacuum in each of us. Unless
we fill it with something, like ignored hunger pains it

will crave God with increasing passion. All too frequently, we try to fill this void with something less than God, but nothing else fits or truly satisfies that longing. Only the living God can fulfill the deep longing of the human spirit. God, Who created that strong desire, has also created a satisfaction for that appetite by making Himself available to the seeking person. Through the prophet Jeremiah God declared, "You will seek Me and find Me, when you search for Me with your whole heart" (Jeremiah 29:13), and David said, "For this cause everyone who is godly will pray to You, In a time when You may be found" (Psalm 32:6).

God is available. He has revealed Himself to us, and His primary manner of self-revelation is His nature as revealed in His names. Looking forward to God's incarnation in Jesus Christ, the prophet Isaiah wrote: "For unto us a Child is born, Unto us a Son is given; And the government will be upon His shoulder. And His name will be called Wonderful, Counselor, Mighty God, Everlasting Father, Prince of Peace" (Isaiah 9:6). What an unfolding of His nature these names afford! Similarly, just before Christ's birth, the angel announced His name to be *Immanuel* [God with us] and *Jesus* [savior]. Long before Jesus ever preached His first message, we were beginning to get acquainted with Him through His assigned names.

The same principle holds true of the Old Testament revelation of God, for God revealed His essential nature to men through His names, especially the compound names for God. It is likely that this was an important source of David's knowledge of God. David put extreme trust in the name of God, even declaring, "Those who know Your name will put their trust in You" (Psalm 9:10), and, "Our heart shall rejoice in Him, Because we have trusted in His holy name" (Psalm 33:21). In fact, David actually worshiped the name of God.

CHAPTER 3

David Worshiped
the Name of God

Our mental concept of God consistently establishes the level of our worship. No one knows all there is to know of God, and some persons have very distorted views of God which restrict their worship. Jesus said to the Samaritan woman, "You worship what you do not know; we know what we worship" (John 4:22). It is probable that He could make that same statement to many individuals and churches today! Understanding just Who God is, therefore, becomes essential if we truly desire to worship Him "in Spirit and in truth" (John 4:24).

Many persons shroud God in secular or political terms, some hold Him distant and beyond reach, and still others approach Him only through some sacred religious trappings. In contrast to this, others have brought God down to their conceptual levels while trying to define God in terms of their educated enlightenment and theological definitions. While condemning the heathen for worshiping a carved idol, they, in turn, worship a self-created idea as their god.

I have counseled many people severely limited in their understanding of God's mercy, compassion, love, and even His gentleness because their earthly fathers had been harsh, unloving, or even cruel. In going from the earthly father to the heavenly Father, they assumed, often subconsciously, that God is like man. They failed to realize that divine redemption seeks to make man more like God.

David wrote, "As a father pities his children, so the LORD pities those who fear [Dutch Bible *praise*] Him, for He knows our frame; He remembers that we are dust" (Psalm 103:13-14).

Realizing our incapacity to know Him, God has mercifully accepted the responsibility of revealing Himself to us. One of His methods is to let us view incorrect concepts of God through the experiences of others. Often a negative experience is more dynamic than a positive one. Remember that God trained David under a rejected King Saul. It was as though God said to David, "That's the way *not* to do it." Perhaps as many children have grown up to despise drinking because of alcoholic parents as those who became drinkers because of the example. Seeing the evil results of wrongdoing is often a forceful deterrent to imitation.

Perhaps this is what God did with Cain's example of improper worship. The lessons it taught certainly reached far beyond his immediate family, for the New Testament refers to it twice (see 1 John 3:12; Jude 11). This experiment of worshiping out of self-will rather than in obedience to the revealed will of God may well have become a negative example for King David, for he had access to the books of Moses which record the unacceptable worship of Cain, Adam's first son.

In his book, *What Happened to Worship*, A. W. Tozer wrote: "The kind of worship Cain offered to God has three basic and serious shortcomings.

"First is the mistaken idea that God is a different kind of God than what He really is. This has to do with the person and character of the sovereign and holy God. How can anyone ever worship God acceptably without knowing what kind of God He really is? Cain surely did not know the true character of God. Cain did not believe that the matter of man's sin was eternally important to God.

"Second is the mistake of thinking that man holds a relationship to God that in fact he does not have. Cain casually assumed that he was deserving of acceptance by the Lord without any intermediary. He refused to accept the judgement of God that man had been alienated from God by sin.

"Third, Cain ... mistakenly assumed that sin is far less serious than it really is." (page 41, Christian Publications, Camp Hill, PA. c. 1985.)

David must have learned from this, for he was consistently cautious to view God as sovereign and holy. Second, David worked on his relationship with God. He did not presume, but he pressed for higher and higher relationships. Furthermore, David viewed sin as serious — both to himself and to God. His answer to sin was confession of his perversity and acceptance of God's provision of cleansing.

To truly know Who God was, David praised the name of God and led others into this practice. In the closing days of his reign, when he was delivering the plans for the Temple to his son Solomon, David offered this prayer of thanksgiving: "Blessed are You, LORD

God of Israel, our Father, forever and ever. Yours, O LORD, is the greatness, the power and the glory, the victory and the majesty; for all that is in heaven and in earth is Yours; Yours is the kingdom, O LORD, and You are exalted as head over all. In Your hand is power and might. In Your hand it is to make great and to give strength to all. Now therefore, our God, we thank You and *praise Your glorious name"* (1 Chronicles 29:10-13, *italics* added).

God's Name is Excellent

This fitting exhortation to the leaders of Israel as David crowned Solomon king over the realm was timely, yet it was by no means a new concept for him. A much younger David had earlier declared, "O LORD, our LORD, how excellent is Your name in all the earth" (Psalm 8:1). Whenever the Old Testament contains the word *LORD*, in all capital letters, it is a euphemism for *YHWH*, the "secret name of God." The Jews considered the divine name too sacred to be pronounced out loud. It is likely that this concept came from an over-application of the commandment, "You shall not take the name of the LORD your God in vain, for the LORD will not hold him guiltless who takes His name in vain" (Exodus 20:7). The Jews feared that mispronouncing God's sacred name would be taking it in vain. Since the name contained neither vowels nor breathing points, it was impossible to know how to correctly pronounce it.

This hallowed view of YHWH carried over into the writing of this name. When scribes transcribed the Bible by hand, they viewed this tetragrammaton, as the theologians call these four consonants, as being so sacred that they would bathe themselves, put on fresh clothes and cut a new quill before writing YHWH.

Then that quill was destroyed, as it was too sacred to use for mere common words. Because of the sacredness of YHWH, the scribes and scholars began substituting a euphemism (a softer word placed in substitution for a harsher word). Whether God wanted this extreme veneration or not we do not know, but it does reveal the hallowed attitude these ancient ones had for their revealed God.

This tetragrammaton occurs 6,800 times in the Bible. Some scholars declare that it is the only name of God in the Bible that refers to Him in essence. They suggest that all other names of God refer to something that He does. Our English Bibles usually translate YHWH as "Jehovah," but if the original language uses the euphemistic word, they translate it as LORD. Whenever we see the capitalized word LORD in our English translations of the Old Testament, we are aware that this is a euphemism for YHWH, the sacred name of Jehovah God.

David declared that this name was excellent. The Hebrew word he used is *addiyr,* which means "large, powerful, famous, gallant, glorious, lordly, noble or worthy." If the Greek language had been available to David instead of the limited Hebrew language, he probably would have piled word upon word trying to build a mountain of descriptive adjectives to express the magnitude and magnificence of God's divine name, for David knew well that God had chosen to reveal His essential nature in His revealed names.

In calling God's name excellent, David may have been remembering the words of Elihu spoken to the suffering Job. He said, "With God is awesome majesty. As for the Almighty, we cannot find Him; He is excellent in power, In judgment and abundant in justice; He does not oppress. Therefore men fear Him;

He shows no partiality to any who are wise of heart"
(Job 37:22-24). The Hebrew word used here is *saggiy,*
which means "mighty, great, excellent." It is derived
from the root word *saga,* which means "to grow, to
cause to enlarge, or, figuratively, to laud."

There can be no doubt that David considered God
mighty, great, and laudable. The more he came to
know God, the more highly David praised and mag-
nified Him, both privately and publicly. The very
name of God unfolded His greatness.

Since God has chosen to reveal Himself to us in His
name, David had good reason to declare that God's
excellence was in His name. Old Testament characters
were said to "live in their names," for those names so
often unveiled the character of the person. For instance,
the name *Jacob* means "supplanter, trickster." Jacob,
the man, was all of this in his relationship with his
father and his father-in-law. Similarly, *Nabal* means
"stupid, wicked, vile." In returning evil for all the good
David had done for him, Nabal proved that he really
did live in his name. We glean much spiritual truth by
checking into the meaning of a person's name. These
names often reveal the fundamental nature of the
person, which gives us insight into the motivation
behind their actions. Similarly, God has capsulized His
nature, His glory and His excellence into the meaning
of His name. His name is one of His methods of causing
us to understand Him.

God's Name is Revealing

God has, indeed, chosen to use His name to unveil
His character to those He loves. When He commissioned
Moses to go to Pharaoh with the message, "Let My
people go," Moses wanted to know "Who shall I say sent
me?" God's answer was, "Thus you shall say to the

children of Israel, 'I AM has sent me to you' " (Exodus 3:14). It is likely that tradition, passed down by word of mouth, had told David that God spoke more than this into the spirit of Moses, for when God speaks, we always hear more in our spirit than our brain translates into language. Perhaps God said, "I can be no less than I am, and I need be no more than I am. What I am is enough. You do not need to beg me to do or be more than I am, because what I am, I am."

Maybe God reminded Moses of what He later proved to David: "I am what I am quite apart from what you are." How easy it is to view God as a glorified perfect Person and limit Him to what our minds can conceive, but God is so far above and beyond us that our minds cannot comprehend Him. David used the imagery of the heavens being higher than the earth as illustrative of how much higher God's nature is than ours. As exaggerated as this is, it still fails to picture the greatness of our God in comparison to the puniness of mankind.

The explanation "I AM" would automatically include God living in an eternal "now." He has always been "I AM;" He will always be "I AM," and right now God is "I AM." Few of us have difficulty believing that in the past, God has been the "I AM," nor do we have much difficulty believing that in the future, He shall be the great "I AM." We do, however, have difficulty in accepting that at this very moment, God is everything that He ever has been or ever will be.

God is not imprisoned with us in our time/space capsule — He lives in eternity where there are no variables. Not only does God not change; He *cannot* change. He Himself declares, "For I am the LORD, I do not change" (Malachi 3:6). What He was, He is and always will be. The New Testament testifies, "Jesus

Christ is the same yesterday, today, and forever"
(Hebrews 13:8). Little wonder that David got so excited
over the name of God, for he could find in it a
revelation of God's unchanging nature.

In the complexity of our religious concepts, we often
fail to see that all God really wants to do is be Himself.
He doesn't want to be what we want Him to be; He
wants to be Himself! We tend to limit God to the area of
revelation we have received. God's grief with Israel's
departure from Himself was that He couldn't have
fellowship with those He loved. Similarly, the grief of
God today is that something keeps us from having
fellowship with Him. Not just sin, but the absence of
praise — the failure to understand the place of praise in
fellowship with God.

In spite of God's being what He is (I AM) everywhere
He is, He isn't being what He is in our lives unless we
are praising Him for Who He really is. One time the
Spirit of the Lord spoke through David, saying "Whoever offers praise glorifies Me; and to him who orders
his conduct aright I will show the salvation of God"
(Psalm 50:23). The Hebrew word we have translated as
"glorifies" is *kabed,* which fundamentally means
"make weighty." What could God mean by, "Whoever
offers praise makes Me weighty?" Let me illustrate it.

No matter how dry the weather has been, in the
atmosphere around us is moisture in the form of
invisible vapor. The meteorologists call this humidity.
In their weather reports, they give this as a percentage
figure. In the same report, they frequently give us a
temperature reading which they call the "dew point,"
which is the temperature at which this invisible moisture will condense and descend on the earth as dew. All
it takes to make this invisible moisture become visible

dew is a decrease in the temperature of the earth's surface.

The minor prophet Hosea concluded his book with the plea, "O Israel, return to the LORD your God ... take words with you, and return to the LORD. Say to Him ... 'we will offer the sacrifices of our lips' " (Hosea 14:2). The New Testament book of Hebrews quotes this passage and calls it "the sacrifice of praise to God, that is, the fruit of our lips, giving thanks to His name" (Hebrews 13:15). In response to this call to return with words of praise, God promised three things: "I will heal their backsliding, I will love them freely ... I will be *like the dew* to Israel" (Hosea 14:4-5, *italics* added).

When those who are in a covenant relationship with God lift their voices in praise to God, their words cool the temperature of their hearts. This causes them to reach the dew point in their relationship with God. This spiritual dew point condenses God's Presence — makes God weighty — much as dew is water vapor made heavy in the early morning. Praising God brings a revelation of God's Presence — it makes God "weighty." Our praise makes visible what was already present, but it was both unseen and unusable. We don't doubt God's assurance, "Lo, I am with you always, even to the end of the age" (Matthew 28:20), but we live most of our lives without a strong awareness of that Presence. When we bring our conscious minds away from the affairs of life to begin to praise the Lord, like condensing dew, God's Presence becomes valid, valuable, and vital. What was formerly a matter of faith now enters the realm of fact which affects our feelings.

How quickly we believers forget that the link between what God really is and what He can be in us is the relationship of praise and worship. It is when we praise God that we release Him to work in our lives.

Furthermore, it is what we praise God for that shapes our concepts of God and releases that aspect of His nature to become active in our lives. God doesn't demand worship because He has an insatiable ego. He calls us to worship Him because that enables Him to be what He is among those He loves. Praise consistently produces a consciousness of God's Presence, and it enlarges our understanding of His Person. Praising children often know God better than nonpraising theologians. Try it!

God's Name is Powerful

Having declared that God's name is excellent, David added, "Out of the mouths of babes and infants You have ordained strength" (Psalm 8:2). When Jesus quoted this verse, in Matthew 21:15, He substituted the word "praise" for "strength," and the Hebrew word for strength allows this. It is not "out of the mouths of pastors and seminary professors," but, "out of the mouths of babes and infants." Jesus said that praising God's name made God's strength available even to the most immature in Christ. It is not our mental knowledge of God that releases His strength, but our vocal praising the name and nature of God that releases the ability of God on our behalf. God's name is powerful, and that strength is available to the weakest saint on earth through the channel of praise.

David certainly knew there was strength in praising the name of the LORD, for this was his regular practice. Listen to him: "I ... will sing praise to *the name* of the LORD Most High" (Psalm 7:17). "I will sing praise to *Your name,* O Most High" (Psalm 9:2). "Give unto the LORD the glory due to *His name*" (Psalm 29:2). "Sing praise to the LORD, you saints of His, and give thanks at the remembrance of *His holy name*"

(Psalm 30:4). "Oh, magnify the LORD with me, and let us exalt *His name* together" (Psalm 34:3). "In God we boast all day long, and praise *Your name* forever" (Psalm 44:8). "According to *Your name,* O God, so is Your praise to the ends of the earth" (Psalm 48:10). "I will praise *Your name,* O LORD, for it is good" (Psalm 54:6). "I will lift up my hands in *Your name*" (Psalm 63:4), and "Sing out the honor of *His name;* make His praise glorious" (Psalm 66:2; all *italics* have been added). Again and again, David praised the name of the LORD rather than merely praising God. David understood there was strength in God's name, and this strength was available to him through praise.

In praising the name of our God, we release Him to be in us what He is, that He "may silence the enemy and the avenger" (Psalm 8:2). Recognizing God to be Who He says He is in our praise releases Him to function in ways consistent with His nature.

If the kitchen sink gets stopped up beyond what a plunger or Drano can handle, we go to the yellow pages of the phone directory and look up "plumbing." We run our fingers down the ads until we find one that says "John Jones — plumber. I specialize in home plumbing problems." Going to the phone, we call the number listed in the ad, and we ask him to come to our house. When he arrives, he fixes the plumbing. Why is he able to do that for us? Because our phone call praised him for being what he said he was in the yellow pages. In praising him, we released him to be what he said he was in our time of need.

When we face a problem in life that is beyond our abilities, we need to turn to the "white pages" of God's Word and find the advertisement which announces that God is available to meet that need. "Call upon Me in the day of trouble; I will deliver you, and you shall glorify Me," God said (Psalm 50:15). Our very call becomes praise, for it is a vocal recognition of His ability and His availability in the midst of our inability.

David learned that when he recognized God to be what the Scriptures declared Him to be, he released God to function for him in all of his circumstances. God revels in being free to be Who He is in relationship to His children. Praising the name of God releases the nature of God on our behalf. It invites Him into our lives to be and do for us what we are unable to be and do for ourselves.

Little wonder, then, that David would sing, "I will praise You, O LORD, with my whole heart; I will tell of all Your marvelous works. I will be glad and rejoice in You; I will sing praise to Your name, O Most High" (Psalm 9:1-2), and "Let all those rejoice who put their trust in You; let them ever shout for joy, because You defend them; let those also who love Your name be joyful in You" (Psalm 5:11).

David learned the value of worshiping the name of God. As David matured in his worship, he became quite specific in his worship of the name of God, for he realized that God had revealed Himself in many compound or covenant names.

CHAPTER 4

David Worshiped God as His Provider

Jehovah-Jireh

David, like many of us, knew extreme contrasts in his life-style. We first meet him as the humble shepherd lad subsisting on the meager fare allotted to him. Later he lived in the palace with the king and ate at his table. Then, for a painful period, he survived in the wilderness, hiding in caves and living off the land while Saul sought him with his army. After Saul's death, David reigned over Judah for seven years, and for the next 33 years he ruled all of Israel. Like Paul, he could say, "I know how to be abased, and I know how to abound. Everywhere and in all things I have learned both to be full and to be hungry, both to abound and to suffer need" (Philippians 4:12).

Still, in all of this, David consistently saw God as the source to meet his needs. In one of his songs, he sang, "You, O LORD, are the portion of my inheritance and my cup; you maintain my lot. The lines have fallen to

me in pleasant places; yes, I have a good inheritance"
(Psalm 16:5-6), and in a more familiar Psalm, he wrote,
"Bless the LORD, O my soul, and forget not all His
benefits ... Who satisfies your mouth with good things,
so that your youth is renewed like the eagle's" (Psalm
103:2,5). Even in the overall scheme of nature, David
saw the hand of God. He sang, "You crown the year
with Your goodness, and Your paths drip with abundance. They drop on the pastures of the wilderness, and
the little hills rejoice on every side. The pastures are
clothed with flocks; the valleys also are covered with
grain; they shout for joy, they also sing" (Psalm 65:11-
13). In Psalm after Psalm, David credits God with
providing all the necessities of life, and he praises God
as the provider.

David made no pretense of having made a covenant
with God for this provision. He merely entered into a
covenant that God had already made with Israel
through Abraham. David was a firm believer that
God's covenants were perpetual. He embraced the
words recorded by another psalmist: "My covenant I
will not break, Nor alter the word that has gone out of
My lips. Once I have sworn by My holiness; I will not lie
to David" (Psalm 89:34-35). David did not discover that
God was our provider; he delighted in this revelation,
and he knew that the first revelation of this facet of
God's nature came to Abraham.

It is likely that David told and retold this story to the
men who gathered with him during his flight from
Saul, for Abraham, the recognized father of the Israelite
nation, was definitely their hero. Abraham learned
what many Israelite leaders later learned: that God
revealed Himself by placing individuals or the entire
nation into problems and then giving them a compound
name for Himself that became a covenant name of

God. This name of God was an unveiling of another aspect of God's inherent nature. When they responded worshipfully to God in this new name, they found their way out of their problem.

David probably found that since God is unchanging, he needed to learn to fall in love with problems instead of dreading and fearing them. He came to see them as altars of worship that allowed God to get into his life. Likely he taught his men that if God is Who He says He is, nothing ought to bother them as long as they were living in what He is! However, no one is living experientially in what God is until they are praising Him for what He is. It is praising God's revealed nature that brings believers into His reliable covenants.

David did not need to tell these rugged men that God called Abraham out of Ur of Chaldees into the land that was now their home, nor did he need to remind them that Abraham was childless. Still, God promised Abraham progeny as the stars of the heavens or as the dust of the earth. God even went so far as to tell Abraham, "You shall be a father of many nations" (Genesis 17:4), and, "In you all the nations shall be blessed" (Galatians 3:8). In spite of his 100 years of age, "Abraham believed God, and it was accounted to him for righteousness" (Galatians 3:6). In response to God's promise and Abraham's faith, God gave him *one* son — Isaac. No more sons were born to Abraham and Sarah. How difficult it must have been for Abraham to see this single son as the fulfillment of the grand promises God had made. How could one son bless all of the nations of the earth?

Most of us have learned that God views His promises on a far different scale than we do. When God speaks to us, we expect immediate and complete fulfillment of all that He has said. We are unable to see the time span in God's plan or the processes He will use to bring about His purposes. We also ignore the many changes that God produces in us before He dares to completely give us what He has promised. Abraham received the beginning of God's promises, but that beginning looked mighty small. It was only a "security payment," or a "guarantee deposit" for him. God usually intervenes in our affairs with small beginnings, but we should rejoice in the day of beginnings, for they are the assurance that more is coming, and God habitually saves the best for the last.

Jehovah's Test

Even though Isaac was the only hope Abraham had of seeing God's promise come to pass, there came a day when God tested Abraham. He said, "Take now your son, your only son Isaac, whom you love, and go to the land of Moriah, and offer him there as a burnt offering on one of the mountains of which I shall tell you" (Genesis 22:2). What a test! Isaac was the channel through which God was expected to fulfill His promise. It seemed inconceivable that Jehovah was asking Abraham to offer Isaac as a human sacrifice, but that is exactly what God said.

Perhaps David emphasized to the men under his command that all it takes to make idolaters of any of us is to make something that is a means become an end. Isaac, the beloved son, was only a means God would use to produce the promised end. Abraham needed to know whether he loved that means more than the promised end.

It is such a subtle shift to embrace the means instead of the end that people often do not realize that it is happening. At the present, I watch many persons worshiping praise and praising worship instead of praising and worshiping God. The means — praise and worship — has replaced the end — responding to God. Maybe we need to take our "only son" to a mountain of God's choosing and offer him unto the Lord so we can get back to the exclusive worship of God.

David, who needed to develop loyalty in his amassing army of distressed persons, probably emphasized heavily that God was helping Abraham to determine who he loved the most. If Abraham had loved Isaac more than he loved his God, Isaac would have become his god. Realistically, that which becomes the focus of our affections becomes the god of our lives. Worship is the expression of an attitude; it is love responding to love. No matter what our lips may say, it is the object of our affections that will receive the worship. I have watched people worship with fervency and affection, but the Holy Spirit has made me aware that the real object of their worship was a recently purchased automobile, an earthly lover, a family relationship, or financial security. While all of their bodily actions seemed to flow to God, and their words were certainly worshipful expressions, none of this was ascending to the Lord Jesus Christ. Their affections were responding to something far beneath God. They worshiped a gift instead of the Giver, or they worshiped love instead of the God Who is love. At the highest level, they may have been worshiping the means instead of the end. They were embracing Isaac instead of Jehovah.

David needed men whose vision remained vital, whose commitment was continual and whose obedience was ongoing. By emphasizing that God desires this same constancy, David was able, through the story of Abraham, to instill in his men a commitment to hold fast to first consecrations.

Only with their imaginations could David's 400 men

enter into the inner struggle and pain Abraham must have felt during the three day journey to the mountain of God's choosing. In coming to David, these men knew loneliness and separation from friends and family, but they were not asked to sacrifice their only sons to Jehovah. All generations of believers have learned that it is one thing to say "yes" to God, but it is totally another thing to actually do what that "yes" demands.

"My only son," Abraham may have mused. "God wants me to kill my only son, Isaac. Why didn't he ask for Ishmael? That would have been so much easier. Why didn't God simply say, 'Take your son?' Then I could have chosen between them. Besides, why does God call Isaac my *only* son? He is actually my second son."

This statement not only bothered Abraham, but it was likely a source of confusion to David's men as well. They, and we, tend to forget that Ishmael was a work of Abraham's flesh for which he repented before God, and the Scriptures teach that when sin is confessed with repentance, God cleanses and removes it from our lives. God says He "will again have compassion on us, and will subdue our iniquities. [He] will cast all our sins into the depths of the sea" (Micah 7:19), and to Isaiah He said, "Your iniquity is taken away, and your sin is purged" (Isaiah 6:7). To all of us, He said, "I, even I, am He who blots out your transgressions for My own sake; and I will not remember your sins" (Isaiah 43:25), and the faith-filled response of forgiven ones is, "You have lovingly delivered my soul from the pit of corruption, for You have cast all my sins behind Your back" (Isaiah 38:17). Paul expressed it this way: "You ... He has made alive together with Him, having forgiven you all trespasses, having wiped out the handwriting of requirements that was against us, which was contrary to us. And He has taken it out of the way, having nailed it to the cross."

Confessed sin results in a cleansed life. God removes the sin from us and removes the record of sin in heaven's book. It is like telling a computer to delete a program. Likely, the monitor will display the message, "Delete this file?" When the operator keys in a "y" for yes, the computer erases the program by blocking all access to that area of memory. The operator is unable to call the program back to the screen. "If we confess our sins, He is faithful and just to forgive us our sins and to cleanse us from all unrighteousness" (1 John 1:9). Heaven deletes all files of our sin, so God is unable to call back to His, or our, attention anything that has been confessed and cleansed.

In God's records, Abraham had but one son, Isaac, for when Abraham confessed the sin of trying to fulfill God's promise through fleshly means, God erased it from the records. When heaven's computer displayed Abraham's file, it listed Abraham as having but one son — Isaac. Little wonder, then, that David could tell his men, "Blessed is he whose transgression is forgiven, whose sin is covered. Blessed is the man to whom the LORD does not impute iniquity, and in whose spirit there is no guile" (Psalm 32:1-2). The confessed works of our flesh, our "Ishmaels," no longer stand against us in heaven's records. God views our righteousness in Christ Jesus rather than the unrighteousness of our flesh. Heaven will not be the unveiling of our failures; it will be the rewarding of our faith.

Jehovah-Jireh

David's men knew well the story of Abraham leaving the two servants at the base of the mountain while he and Isaac carried the wood and the firepot to the top. Having built a crude altar of natural stones, Abraham bound Isaac and laid him upon the wood while explaining what God had required of him. As Abraham's shaky hand drew back the knife for the death plunge, "The angel of the LORD called to him from heaven and said, 'Abraham, Abraham! ... Do not lay your hand on the lad, or do anything to him; for now I know that you fear God, since you have not withheld your son, your only son, from Me' " (Genesis 22:11-12).

Immediately, the angel directed Abraham's attention to a ram caught in a thicket of brush by its horns. This became the substitute lamb, a beautiful type of Christ Jesus, Who took our place upon the altar as "The Lamb of God which takes away the sins of the world" (John 1:29). Abraham barely got the ram on the altar when God revealed Himself as *JEHOVAH-JIREH*, "The LORD-Will-Provide" (Genesis 22:14). This was the very first covenant name that God had given to mankind, and it revealed His tender care and constant provision for His children.

David probably explained to his men that *JIREH* means more than "to provide." It literally means "to see" or "to foresee." Even our English word *provide* indicates this. It comes from two Latin words: *pro*, which means "beforehand," as in *prologue*; and *vide*, which means "to see," as in *video*. *Jehovah-Jireh*, then, is one who foresees, or sees well in advance.

Jehovah-Jireh stood at the beginning of history and saw all history as though it were present, and God saw to everything He saw. There wasn't anything He saw that He didn't see to, so we need not get nervous over anything that we just now see. Nothing catches God off guard. He never has had to say "oops" over anything that has happened in human history. We get unreasonably excited over unforeseen events, and we give God this "unknown information" abundantly and emotionally. In response to our worried prayers, God answers, "I knew it was coming. I took care of it long ago. Look in the thicket and you'll find my provision. I am *Jehovah-Jireh,* you know."

Those who have a problem with the foreknowledge of God need to remember that salvation preceded sin. Jesus is "The lamb slain from the foundation of the world" (Revelation 13:8) Who "... chose us in Him before the foundation of the world, that we should be holy and without blame before Him in love" (Ephesians 1:4). Sin did not force God to go to "plan B," for God saw men in sin long before He laid the foundations of this world. At that moment, He made ample provision for sinning persons. God provided the cross before He created the first man. *Jehovah-Jireh* is from one extreme of eternity to the other. He sees — He foresees — and He sees for everything that He sees. He is *Jehovah-Jireh,* our provider!

David and his men needed to learn everything they could from this traumatic experience of Abraham, for they, too, faced testings. As they followed David when he fled from Saul, they wandered in the wilderness living in caves like animals with no provision for the necessities of life. King Saul declared them to be criminals. This meant that if anyone chose to help them, they became "accessories to the crime." Some might say that these men lived "by their wits," but David declared that they lived by God's hand. He sang, "My praise shall be of You in the great congregation: I will pay My vows before those who fear Him, the poor shall eat and be satisfied; those who seek Him will praise the LORD" (Psalm 22:25-26). David seemed to realize that praising God's name, *Jehovah-Jireh,* brought God's provision — "the poor shall eat." It is imperative that we learn to get the problem and the solution together by praise.

In his beautiful shepherd's Psalm, David said, "I shall not want ... You prepare a table before me in the presence of my enemies" (Psalm 23:1,5). Even when fleeing from Saul, David visualized himself as under the protectorate care of the Great Shepherd Who had led His people through the wilderness for forty years while providing them with water, fresh manna and occasional quail. David felt that if God could do that for the millions under Moses, He could certainly provide the food, clothing, and water he and his 400 men needed. We have no record of David begging God to meet those temporal needs. He believed that praising God's marvelous name as the Provider for His children was enough.

David came to the throne in good health, and he brought his men with him. Many of them achieved status as "mighty men" or "men of renown," and he gave them special positions in the kingdom. God's provision for them carried right into their aging years. God foresaw their needs, oversaw their lives, and saw for all of their temporal needs when they learned to praise Him as *Jehovah-Jireh.*

During the years of wandering, David needed more than food and water — he needed help in many different ways. In remembrance of this, "David spoke to the LORD the words of this song, on the day when the LORD had delivered him from the hand of all his enemies, and from the hand of Saul. And he said: 'The LORD is my rock, my fortress and my deliverer; the God of my strength, in Him I will trust, My shield and the horn of my salvation, my stronghold and my refuge; my Savior, You save me from violence. I will call upon the LORD, who is worthy to be praised; so shall I be saved from my enemies' " (2 Samuel 22:1-4).

David praised the LORD for being his rock, fortress, deliverer, strength, shield, horn (strength), stronghold, refuge and Savior. All of this, and more, is encompassed in the covenant provision of *Jehovah-Jireh*. As David and his men praised *Jehovah-Jireh*, God became the source of their every provision: body, soul, and spirit. And so He will for us!

This consistent intervention of God as the source of provision enhanced David's awareness that the God he served was a *living God*. *Jehovah-Jireh* translated beautifully into "God is alive and well!" What an undergirding for worship this became to David and will be to us.

As David matured in his relationship with God, he found other covenants God had made with His people. These were as applicable to his specific needs as the covenant of *Jireh*. It is clear that David learned to praise the Lord as his healer, time after time.

CHAPTER 5

David Worshiped God
as His Healer

Jehovah-Rapha

David was not only a lover of God, he was equally a seeker after God. He wrote, "When You said, 'Seek My face,' my heart said to You, 'Your face, LORD, I will seek' " (Psalm 27:8). In his seeking after God, one would expect David to look into the writing of Moses to learn what God had revealed to him. That he did this is seen in his statement: "He made known His ways to Moses, His acts to the children of Israel" (Psalm 103:7). God declared His purposes to Moses before He did anything among the Hebrews, but the children of Israel recognized the hand of God only after the deed was done. Moses had come to know the ways of God, so he was involved with God both in faith and in action. David coveted this for his life, too. He was never content to know God by looking backwards; he wanted to know God in the present.

David was not only a seeker after truth; he was a

communicator of truth. In his songs and Psalms, he consistently taught others what he had learned about God from the observation of the lives of others and by his personal experiences with the living God he loved and served. When the memory of his escape from Abimelech was still fresh in his mind, David wrote, "Come, you children, listen to me; I will teach you the fear of the LORD" (Psalm 34:11). At another time, after talking about being forgiven for the iniquity of his sin, David said, "I will instruct you and teach you in the way you should go; I will guide you with My eye" (Psalm 32:8).

When David was formulating his fledgling army during the years he was in exile from the palace, it is likely that he took the role of an instructor on regular occasions. It is not difficult to visualize David recounting the stories of Moses and the Israelites as they had their wilderness experiences. At night around the campfire, David dramatically recounted some of those events. Although story-telling may be a lost art in our generation of television, it was the main form of entertainment in days gone by. David, who had spent much time musing on these happenings during his days as a shepherd, had probably polished his ability to dramatize these stories until his listeners found themselves transported to the desert sands with Moses.

The Release

Perhaps one of his favorite stories was the crossing through the Red Sea by the recently released slaves from Egypt. These Hebrews came out of Egypt with much jubilation following their 400-year sojourn there. During three hundred of those four hundred years, they had been slaves to the Egyptians. On Passover night, God set them free, and the Egyptians urged them to leave the land. On their backs and in carts, they carried all their earthly possessions that were movable. Also, they joyfully carried immense riches which they had received from the Egyptians as 300 years' back wages, plus interest. The uncontrolled march ceased when they reached the Red Sea, for they could find no way to cross it. Setting up a temporary camp, they cried to Moses, who, in turn, called upon God for further deliverance. God sent an east wind to blow across the water all night long. Hour by hour, the wind cut a progressively deeper path in the sea. While this was happening, God placed His brilliant pillar of flame over the Red Sea so the people could watch this gradual miracle.

By the time Pharaoh discovered the Hebrews were trapped by the sea, he had already repented of having released these slaves. He had not anticipated the economic havoc in Egypt the loss of the Hebrews would cause. This relentless ruler of Egypt saw this circumstance as his last opportunity to force these people to return to servitude. Quickly rallying his army, he led his crack troop of charioteers in pursuit of his former slaves.

Mercifully, the God Who was Light to the Hebrews chose to become Darkness to the Egyptians, and they were forced to stop their charge while waiting for daylight. As the east wind completed a pathway through the sea, God told Moses to lead the people to the far side. In spite of what they had witnessed, they were still doubtful that the walls of water would remain in their present upright position. Their fear of what might happen prevented them from entering into what had already happened, for fear always contends with faith.

When this multitude of people refused to walk through the water with Moses, Jehovah lifted the darkness from over the Egyptian army and let them see the dilemma. It didn't take them long to get their chariots moving toward the millions of people now trapped between their fear of the water and their terror of their former oppressors. The sound of the whirling chariot wheels, many of which had knife blades sticking out of the spokes, struck terror in the hearts of these people. They rushed like a mob through the pathway in the sea. The great faith chapter of the Bible says, "By faith they passed through the Red Sea as by dry land, whereas the Egyptians, attempting to do so, were drowned" (Hebrews 11:29). They went through by faith, all right — faith that the Egyptians would slaughter, torture, and capture them. But at least that is faith; God used Pharaoh to get them through the sea.

David couldn't help highly dramatizing the story of this mad rush through the sea's channel ahead of the hot pursuit of the Egyptian charioteers. Amazingly enough, the sea bed was dry for the Hebrews to run through, but it became as soft as quicksand once the Egyptian chariots drove on it. The chariots not only got stuck, but the wheels of the chariots twisted off as the horses pulled one way and then another in a futile effort to get the chariots loose.

The mighty hand of God that had opened the sea now closed it quickly upon the Egyptian army, and they all drowned. The Hebrews would never again see their enemies, except to strip armor from the dead bodies that would wash ashore in the coming days.

The Rejoicing

This called for a celebration of a magnitude Israel had never before experienced. Moses wrote a song which the congregation sang, and Miriam, his sister, "took the timbrel in her hand; and all the women went out after her with timbrels and with dances" (Exodus 15:20). What a display of relief, joy, and freedom this became. Song, dance, and feasting were the order of the day, and this festivity continued for two or three days. There is no celebration that equals that of captives set free.

Such enthusiastic worship produces thirst, and there was no drinking water available in the immediate vicinity of the Red Sea. Eventually, scouts returned to report there was water at Marah, about three days' journey away. Unpleasantly, the water was brackish. To dehydrated people, even brackish water is preferred to thirst, so the celebrants headed for Marah in more of a rout than a march. It was each person for him or herself.

The Test

This multitude of people, variously estimated to be from one and a half to four and a half million people, quickly slaked their thirst at Marah's pool. Very quickly, they discovered the water gave them a severe stomachache. There is a hint in the Hebrew that it actually gave them all diarrhea. What a mess! What misery! "The people murmured against Moses, saying, 'What shall we drink?' " (Exodus 15:24). They left the fresh water of the Nile River in Egypt, and in its place they drank water that was brackish, bitter, and biologically dangerous.

It was a test (see Exodus 15:25), but they did not know it. God had placed them, like Abraham before them, in a difficult circumstance to reveal still another facet of His nature to them. Human nature being what it is, we learn best in the midst of a test.

These people had a very limited concept of God. During the 400 years they lived in Egypt, they had neither an officiating high priest nor an anointed prophet. The last revelation of God had come through Moses as he announced judgment after judgment upon the Egyptians for their disobedience. After seeing these increasingly severe plagues that had come upon Pharaoh and his people, the Hebrews came to believe that God was harsh and austere. They assumed that He quickly and relentlessly punished any and every disobedience to His will.

Perhaps they feared that during their celebration songs and dances they had done something wrong. Maybe they thought they had been too exuberant, or perhaps they questioned the purity of their emotions during part of the rejoicing. Now they were sick, and they believed that they were going to die. They quickly forgot all of God's demonstrated mercy in the midst of their physical agony. Their memories could only recall God's death-dealing plagues upon the Egyptians. They assumed they had escaped the plague of death in Egypt only to experience it in the wilderness.

It is such an unbalanced picture of God that many Christians carry to their graves. David did not want his followers to have such a lopsided view of God. He taught his men, "Many are the afflictions of the righteous, But the LORD delivers him out of them all ... The LORD redeems the soul of His servants, And none of those who trust in Him shall be condemned" (Psalm 34:19, 22). David knew well the judgmental nature of God, but he equally understood the forgiveness and tender mercies of His living God.

In response to the complaints of the people, Moses cried out to God. God answered Moses' hurried prayer by commanding him to cut down a specific tree and cast it into the pool. Abraham had his ram, but Moses had God's desert tree that had been growing alongside that pool for hundreds of years. *Jehovah-Jireh* had provided long before the need arose. When Moses obeyed God and could convince the people to take a second drink (what a salesman), God healed both the pool and the people.

The Revelation — Jehovah-Rapha

Then God said, "If you diligently heed the voice of the LORD your God and do what is right in His sight, give ear to His commandments and keep all His statutes, I will put none of the diseases on you which I have brought on the Egyptians. For I am the LORD who heals you" — *Jehovah-Rapha* (Exodus 15:26).

God was unveiling another aspect of His complex nature. He is a God of vengeance. He did send plague after plague upon the rebellious Egyptians — and He was still capable of doing that — but, He was equally a healing God. Some have translated *Jehovah-Rapha* as, "I am a physician by nature. I can't help Myself." To the rebellious, God may inflict wounds that prove to be incurable. Conversely, for the obedient, the Lord binds up wounds that have been inflicted in life and heals the person, making him or her whole in body, soul, and spirit. The LORD is a physician by nature. He has to override that nature to do anything other than bind up and heal.

Moses sang a prophetic song in his last days. The words, spoken in the voice of God, said: " 'Now see that I, even I, am He, and there is no God besides Me; I kill and I make alive; I wound and I heal; nor is there any who can deliver from My hand' " (Deuteronomy 32:39). This is the balance God wants us to see in His nature. God doesn't want us to see merely the judgmental aspect of His being. God is a merciful Healer as well as the Judge of the earth.

David probably sought to explain to his troops that a person's relationship to God determines whether God is a killer or a healer. Obedience to His commands brings us under the rays of His healing power, but disobedience puts us under the sentence of God. The incident at Marah was an attention-getter that allowed

those newly freed slaves to find another concept of the
Almighty God Who had brought them out of Egypt.
God fully intended to take them into the promised
land. Their walk through the wilderness would be far
more pleasant if they could see God as their Provider
(Jireh) and their Healer *(Rapha)*.

David learned to praise the name of *Jehovah-Rapha*,
for he uses the word *rapha* six or seven times in the
Psalms. One notable occasion is, "O LORD my God, I
cried out to You, and You healed [*rapha*] me. O LORD,
You brought my soul up from the grave; You have kept
me alive, that I should not go down to the pit" (Psalm
30:2-3). David was, of course, far more familiar with the
Hebrew language than most of us are. He knew what
he was declaring. We are more dependent upon the
Hebrew scholars to know the depth of the meaning of
rapha. One of these scholars is William Wilson Kregel
who, in his book *Old Testament Word Studies,* says,
" 'Rapha' means to heal diseases of all kinds, partic-
ularly wounds by outward application, and binding or
sewing; to heal a distressed nation or person by restor-
ing them to prosperous circumstances; to heal in a
moral sense, to cure the mind, to pardon the soul."
(Kregel Publications, Grand Rapids, MI. c. 1978.)

David discovered that our God is all of that. He
declared his conviction that God healed diseases of all
kinds by his statement: "Bless the LORD, O My soul,
And forget not all His benefits; Who forgives all your
iniquities, Who heals all your diseases" (Psalm 103:2-3).
The psalmist also recognized that *Jehovah-Rapha*
bound up specific wounds, for he wrote: "He heals the
broken-hearted And binds up their wounds" (Psalm
147:3). David shows that he knew that *Rapha* healed a
distressed nation and restored them to prosperous
circumstances, for he wrote: "O God, You have cast us

off; You have broken us down; You have been displeased; Oh, restore us again! You have made the earth tremble; You have broken it; Heal [rapha] its breaches" (Psalm 60:1-2). David's understanding of Jehovah's healing in the area of the moral and mental nature shows in his song, "Have mercy on me, O LORD, for I am weak; O LORD, heal [rapha] me, for my bones are troubled. My soul also is greatly troubled" (Psalm 6:2).

The sixth meaning of *rapha* given to us by Wilson Kregel is "to pardon the soul." David had a good grasp on this aspect of God's healing nature. He wrote: "I said, 'LORD, be merciful to me; Heal [rapha] my soul, for I have sinned against You.' " (Psalm 41:4). Every aspect of God's healing nature was clear to David. He had tested and proved that *Jehovah-Rapha* was alive and functioning in David's affairs.

The Application

In the years that David and his troops fled from Saul and contended with surrounding enemies, we do not read of their having a physician among them. It is inconceivable to believe that none of David's men ever got wounded or sick. Surely some of the wives or children needed medical attention occasionally. Did David's telling and retelling of the revelation God gave to Israel and the covenant He made with them there cause these distressed persons to turn to *Jehovah-Rapha* for their healings? It had certainly done that to David.

Whether David knew more about God's covenant of healing than we know is a matter of conjecture. We definitely have more Scriptural teaching than he had, and we have far more Bible examples of God's intervention into the sickness of men and women. Perhaps David, in his simple way of dealing directly with God, was less encumbered with the doctrine of divine healing than we are. Many Christian groups have developed a spiritual dogma about healing, and they have embellished their doctrine with certain necessary rituals in order for the sick to find healing. So be it, if it works.

At Marah, God was revealing to Moses another facet of the divine nature, rather than a doctrine of healing. He was declaring Himself to be a healing God. Obedience to His Words brought healing to the entire nation. They did not seem to have doctrinal practices that had to be performed before God would become to them what He was in His essential being.

Perhaps we need to return to the simplicity of praising God for being Who He declares Himself to be. Maybe when sickness lays hold of us, we need to cool our heated minds with praise to *Jehovah-Rapha* until we reach the spiritual dew-point that will condense the invisible healing nature of God until it distills and settles on the surface of our lives like dew.

To David's credit, we can say that he didn't beg God to be what He was already. He merely praised God for Who He had revealed Himself to be, and entered into the covenant God had made with His covenant people. God did not reveal what He could become. He revealed Who He is already. We praise Him, not to make Him become what we want Him to be, but to release Him to be what He said He is in the midst of our problem.

Although the first Psalm of book five does not have a title, it sounds so much like David that many give him credit for it. In it the psalmist writes, "He sent His word and healed them, and delivered them from their destructions. Oh, that men would give thanks to the Lord for His goodness, and for His wonderful works to the children of men!" (Psalm 107:20-21). David sensed that if God said it, then it was settled, and he believed it. God sent His Word declaring Himself to be their

Physician, and David claimed that promise. Is it possible that we could too?

During the last years of my final pastorate, we had far more persons healed during the praise sessions than had formerly been healed by anointing with oil and laying hands upon them while praying a prayer of faith. Somehow, the simplicity of the sick person praising a healing God got the need and the provision together in a non-threatening way. Almost involuntarily, God's healing flowed into their bodies. We have the option to fix our attention on our pain or to adore our divine Physician with praise. The first merely complicates the problem, while the second often solves it.

The Sovereignty of Jehovah-Rapha

I believe that all of us who have been involved in praying for the sick over the years will admit that what we do not know about divine healing far exceeds what we do know. I can attest that every time I have made a doctrine out of divine healing, it has hindered the flow of this grace of God. It was when I got the sick individual into the Presence of a healing God that marvelous things took place. Perhaps we need to join David in just praising the name of *Jehovah-Rapha.*

Whether or not we fully understand how it works, *Jehovah-Rapha* has revealed Himself to be our Physician. When David's son, born to Bathsheba out of their adulterous relationship, lay dying, "David therefore pleaded with God for the child, and David fasted and went in and lay all night on the ground." For seven days, David interceded with God in a complete fast, but the child died anyway. When David heard that the child was dead, he arose, washed, changed his clothes and went to the house of the LORD and worshiped. When asked about this strange behavior, "He said,

'While the child was alive, I fasted and wept; for I said, "Who can tell whether the LORD will be gracious to me, that the child may live?" But now he is dead; why should I fast? Can I bring him back again? I shall go to him, but he shall not return to me' " (2 Samuel 12:16, 22-23). Although David had caught a glimpse of *Jehovah-Rapha,* he realized what Paul later put in classic prose: "For now we see in a mirror, dimly, but then face to face. Now I know in part, but then I shall know just as I also am known" (1 Corinthians 13:12). The physician nature of Jehovah never violates His sovereignty. What often seems to be an insolvable puzzle will someday be as plain as the noonday sun. It did not weaken David's faith in a living God Who heals when healing did not always come when he requested it. Every time God intervened in David's sickness, it was proof positive that God was alive. It also became a principal reason for worship and praise.

Whether we can fully appropriate the benefits or not, *Jehovah-Rapha* is the Healer for the whole person. He is the Physician to our wounded emotions as well as our sick bodies. He heals the mind twisted by sin and restores it to balanced thinking. God displays an interest in our whole being. He has become the Healer — the Restorer of life in every facet of our being. As David learned in the cave of Adullam, praising God brings healing of the soul's loneliness, depression, anxiety, and fear. *Jehovah-Rapha* can touch these as quickly as He can heal a headache or cancer.

During the long years that David was a military tactician, he was completely happy to have his God as the Physician for the troops, but he was equally glad to have Jehovah as his banner, for without the help of God, David would have lost some very important battles.

CHAPTER 6

David Worshiped God as His Banner

Jehovah-Nissi

Every military tactician studies the battles that others have fought — especially the battles fought on the same geographic territory. David was no exception. It is likely that time and time again, he went over the battles led by Moses and Joshua. He used these battles as training maneuvers for his fighting men. One of these battles that David studied with interest was the battle between Israel and Amalek.

This very first battle that Moses and Joshua fought after leaving Egypt came shortly after Israel's experience at Marah. Amalek fearfully watched this huge multitude of people in the wilderness right at the border of his lands. They were a threat to him. He reasoned that the sooner he attacked them, the better chance he had of defeating them. So without a declaration of war or any diplomatic contact, he marched against Israel with his highly trained army. The dust raised by the marching of thousands of feet alerted Moses to this advancing army. Very likely, Moses went directly to God in prayer, informing God of the imminent attack. "What shall we do?" Moses asked God.

"Go out and fight Amalek," God answered.

"With what?" Moses responded. "I don't have fighting men; I have slaves who have no knowledge of war. Actually, they had never held a sword in their hands until we stripped the slain bodies of Pharaoh's chariot troops who drowned in the Red Sea."

"Meet this attack with your young men. Arm them with those Egyptian weapons," God demanded.

"But God," Moses pled, "I don't have the heart to lead these untrained young men into battle. It would be a slaughter of innocents."

"I don't intend you to lead them," God said. "Send Joshua."

"Oh, God, not the youth pastor," Moses may have said. "He's so young and inexperienced. He has a lot of zeal, but he still lacks a great deal of knowledge. Furthermore, he has absolutely no military experience."

"Send Joshua," God said, "and you take your rod with you to the top of the hill. As you stretch it out, Joshua will be victorious."

Moses obeyed. Joshua advanced and God gave the victory. What a day of triumph it was for Israel! As long as Moses extended the rod, Joshua and his untrained forces drove back the invincible army of Amalek. When Moses' arms got too tired to continue to hold out the rod, he put them down to rest and regain circulation. When the rod was down, Amalek turned the tide of battle in his favor. When Moses re-extended that rod, Joshua regained lost territory. Aaron and Hur, elders who had accompanied Moses up this mountain, saw the dilemma and rolled a large boulder for Moses to sit on. Standing on either side of Moses, they held up his arms until Amalek was ultimately defeated. Like many sincere elders since then, they realized that their leader did not need criticism; he needed help.

David was very familiar with this story, for not only was it recorded in the books of Moses, but it was told in generation after generation as one of the great war stories.

Nissi — Banner of Protection

When the battle was over, God gave Moses another covenant name — *Jehovah-Nissi*: "The LORD our banner" (Exodus 17:15). The banner referred to was the rod Moses had extended over the battlefield. In hand-to-hand combat, a soldier would chase, parry and thrust with his sword, and follow his opponent until he had incapacitated him. This often involved a lengthy conflict during which the battle lines often changed. The victorious soldier didn't want to remain long in enemy territory, so he looked for his "banner," which was usually a highly polished metal emblem fixed to a long pole. The emblem bearer was always at the side of the leader of the battle. That was the place where the action was going on, and it was a place of relative safety. It was here individual soldiers who had become separated from their army in the conflict could assemble for the next thrust of battle.

Very early, God revealed Himself to Israel as their Banner. God was molding this multitude of persons into a nation. In conquering territory to live in, they would fight seven or more nations. They were learning that He would be the Captain of their armies, and He would be the rallying point for their soldiers. Israel was not expected to know much about military tactics, for their expertise was brick-making. Their inexperience was no severe limitation, for their divine Leader knew all that was necessary to know. The "LORD of hosts" had offered Himself as their Banner, and they would march under His direction and His protection. As long as He was extended over their armies, they would be as victorious as Joshua, who won such a triumphant victory over Amalek when Moses extended his rod over the army of Israel.

Isaiah was the channel through whom God declared, "Behold, I will lift My hand in an oath to the nations, and set up My standard for the peoples" (Isaiah 49:22). God placed Himself as the rallying point for the nations of the world, bringing them to Israel. The figure of speech he used was "banner" or "standard."

For years, believers have found comfort in the promise, "When the enemy comes in, like a flood the Spirit of the LORD will raise up a standard [banner] against him" (Isaiah 59:19, punctuated the way the Hebrew rabbis punctuate it). Our defense is as much the upraised banner of God as was Israel's. When the enemy dares to attack, God raises the banner of His Presence over the Christian or the Church. This summons heaven's army [called "the heavenly host"] to rally to the defense. At this point, the message God sent to King Jehoshaphat becomes applicable to us. "Do not be afraid nor dismayed because of this great multitude, for the battle is not yours, but God's" (2 Chronicles 20:15).

The key to victory is running to the Banner. We do not win by calling for the banner to come to us. God extends His banner to direct us to a place of refuge.

How thoroughly David knew this. He consistently spoke of God as his defense in war. He called Jehovah his rock, his high tower, his shield, his buckler, his defense, and many other terms which proved that David knew God was the leader of the army, Who knew that the best defense was a good offense. The same banner that offered refuge also gave direction for battle. God did not forever hide David in a cave. He frequently sent him headlong against the enemy. The same banner that indicates "Here I am" can also signal "Charge!"

We do not know for certain that the Book of Joshua was available to David. What we do know is that with or without the book, David was extremely familiar with the conquest of Canaan under the leadership of Joshua. To the Israelites, this was comparable to George Washington's battle to bring independence to the thirteen colonies. Both nations had their beginnings in wars that seemed impossible to win, but they won!

Joshua served faithfully under Moses for forty years. He is a prime example of a good number two man. Just before he died, Moses laid his hand upon Joshua and transferred all powers of leadership to this man. During the thirty days that Israel mourned the death of Moses, their beloved leader, Joshua was number one in command in Israel. But when God directed them to cross the Jordan River and prepare for conquest, Joshua met the "Commander of the army of the LORD" (Joshua 5:14). Joshua surrendered his command to this Angel of the LORD and became second in command once again.

Nissi — Banner of Direction

Joshua never lost sight of his secondary position as a general of Israel's army. He consistently depended upon the One Who controlled the banner. In my recent book, *Meeting God,* I wrote, "As opposed to the Book of Judges, the Book of Joshua does not hail any heroes.

One would expect to find a national image emerging from so successful a conquest, but even Joshua is not pictured as the glorious conqueror that the judges of a succeeding generation would be. Perhaps it stems from his confrontation with the 'Lord of hosts' right after they crossed Jordan ... from that day on, Joshua did not consider himself as the commander-in-chief of Israel's army, but as an officer who took orders from his superior." (page 10, Creation House. c. 1986.)

Joshua functioned under the banner of Jehovah, and David learned from this action. Consistently, David looked to the LORD for direction in the battles he undertook. He found the wisdom of the LORD to be greatly superior to his own military ability. He wrote, "We will rejoice in your salvation, and in the name of our God we will set up our banners! ... Now I know that the LORD saves His anointed; He will answer him from His holy heaven with the saving strength of His right hand. Some trust in chariots, and some in horses; but we will remember the name of the LORD our God. They have bowed down and fallen; but we have risen and stand upright. Save, LORD!" (Psalm 20:5-9).

Quite obviously, David had learned to praise the name of *Jehovah-Nissi*. He found God to be both his offense and defense. Fleeing to the Banner in praise and rejoicing made all the hosts of heaven available to David — and it does for us, too! God has not guaranteed that the enemy who is against us would be less powerful than we. He has, however, promised to be the extended Banner, or Rod, that brings the heavenly hosts to fight that enemy. We simply need to know what Elisha told his servant when they found themselves surrounded by the Syrian army: " 'Do not fear, for those who are with us are more than those who are with them.' And Elisha prayed, and said, 'LORD, I pray, open his eyes that he may see.' Then the LORD opened the eyes of the young man, and he saw. And behold, the mountain was full of horses and chariots of fire all around Elisha" (2 Kings 6:16-17).

Repeatedly, David faced overwhelming odds in battle, but by putting his confidence in the LORD, his Banner, he won every war he fought. In facing Goliath, he stood alone. It was man-to-man. On one occasion, Jonathan and David took on an entire company of the Philistines, and on another, David and his companion did the same thing. Whether David fought alone, with a companion, with his 300 mighty men or with an entire army, his dependence was always upon the LORD of hosts.

David, like Joshua, learned that battling under the banner of Jehovah called for implicit obedience. There cannot be two supreme commanders in a battle. God tested David on this. Once when David was hiding from Saul, the king entered the cave where David and his men were hiding. As King Saul attended to his needs (1 Samuel 24:3), "the men of David said to him, 'This is the day of which the LORD said to you, "Behold, I will deliver your enemy into your hand, that you may do to him as it seems good to you" ' " (1 Samuel 24:4). With this encouragement, David foresaw an end to the conflict and a shortcut to the throne, but it wasn't God's way. God allowed David to cut off a corner of Saul's robe, but He prevented him from slaying Saul. David told his men, "The LORD forbid ... that I should ... stretch out my hand against him, seeing he is the anointed of the LORD" (1 Samuel 24:6).

Calling to Saul after he left the cave, David showed him the corner of the robe he had cut off, and by this he convinced Saul that he was not in insurrection against

the kingdom. This reprieve proved to be very temporary. Slaying Saul would have been permanent, but
He Who held the banner said "No!," and "no" is a
command, not a suggestion.

On another occasion, David faced another chance to
assassinate Saul. He slipped up on Saul's camp and
found everyone sound asleep. Accompanied by Abishai,
David sneaked into the camp and took Saul's spear and
jug of water. Abishai said to David, "God has delivered
your enemy into your hand this day. Now, therefore,
please, let me strike him at once with the spear, right to
the earth" (1 Samuel 26:8). Again, David had to say,
"The LORD forbid that I should stretch out my hand
against the LORD's anointed" (2 Samuel 26:11).

Perhaps it was at this time that David sang, "Plead
my cause, O LORD, with those who strive with me;
fight against those who fight against me. Take hold of
shield and buckler, and stand up for my help. Also draw
out the spear, and stop those who pursue me. Say to my
soul, 'I am your salvation.' Let those be put to shame
and brought to dishonor who seek after my life ... let the
angel of the LORD chase them ... let the angel of the
LORD pursue them" (Psalm 35:1-6). What God would
not allow David to do, David pled with God to accomplish.

David did not fully understand why God prevented
him from slaying the man who was hunting him like a
wild animal. David did know, however, that God was in
charge of this conflict. This left him with no choice but
to obey the orders of his Superior Officer. After
returning the sword and the water jug to Saul, David
received Saul's promise: "I will harm you no more,
because my life was precious in your eyes this day"
(1 Samuel 26:21). Unable to believe Saul, David fled

to Achish in the land of the Philistines for the second time.

While David was living there, the Philistines went to war against King Saul and Israel. David and his army were invited by Achish to participate as his personal body guards. However, when the lords of the Philistines saw David in their army, they were horrified, and they insisted that David be dismissed. They didn't trust this conqueror of their former champion, Goliath. It was because of David they were in subjection to Israel. The purpose of this war was to break this dominance with military might.

When David returned to his home city of Ziklag, he found that in his absence some Amalekites had burned the city to the ground and had taken the women and children captive. "Then David and the people who were with him lifted up their voices and wept, until they had no more power to weep" (1 Samuel 30:4). The anger and frustration of David's men was so great that they threatened to kill him.

"But David strengthened himself in the LORD his God" (1 Samuel 30:6). David called for Abiathar, the priest, and instructed him to inquire of God whether they should pursue the Amalekites or not. God's answer was "Pursue, for you shall surely overtake them and without fail recover all" (1 Samuel 30:8). Even in the midst of grief and personal loss, David would not operate under his own banner. He wanted directions from *Jehovah-Nissi* — "The Lord-Our-Banner." No wonder David was so successful in battle.

David learned what we, too, must know. Obedience to the Captain of the Heavenly Hosts does not mean inactivity. God directed, and David and his army fought. The defeat of the Amalekites took from twilight of one day until the evening of the next day (1 Samuel

30:17). David recovered everything, but it required a lengthy battle. All during this fight, David envisioned the banner of the Lord stretched out over him directing the battle. Again and again, this was the pattern: God and David working together.

On one occasion, and it could have been this one, David sang, "Blessed be the LORD my Rock, Who trains my hands for war, and my fingers for battle — my lovingkindness and my fortress, my high tower and my deliverer, My shield and the One in whom I take refuge, Who subdues my people under me" (Psalm 144:1-2). David accepted God's strength and training, but he also used them.

How easy it is for us to expect our Captain to also become our foot soldier. We wait for Him to do everything for us, thereby freeing us to be inactive observers, but God expects us to be active in the conflict against sin. God will raise up a standard against our enemy, but we may have to lift a weapon against him.

The New Testament speaks of the Christian life involving wrestling, resisting, and contending. This is active involvement, but when it is directed involvement, we are assured of victory. The promise is "Sin shall not have dominion over you" (Romans 6:14), and "The God of peace will crush Satan *under your feet* shortly" (Romans 16:20; *italics* added.) *Jehovah-Nissi* is still in covenant relationship with His people; they can't fail as long as they stay close to the Banner.

Nissi — Banner of Rejoicing

There are students of the Hebrew language and culture who believe that *Jehovah-Nissi* also implies the idea of exultation and triumph. They visualize flags, banners, and battle standards being waved furiously in proclamation and celebration of victory. David certainly understood this, for he sang, "We will rejoice in your salvation, and in the name of our God we will set up our banners!" (Psalm 20:5). He also affirmed, "You have given a banner to those who fear You, that it may be displayed because of the truth" (Psalm 60:4).

If the celebration David staged for the return of the Ark to Jerusalem is any indication of the way he celebrated God, the victory marches home from the battlefields must have been colorful and resplendent with banners. David was never hesitant to ascribe all victories to Jehovah, and he wanted everyone to join him in his rejoicing. He wrote one song to the Chief Musician that says, "Oh, clap your hands, all you peoples! Shout to God with the voice of triumph! For the LORD Most High is awesome; He is a great King over all the earth. He will subdue the people under us, and the nations under our feet" (Psalm 47:1-3).

David's deep awareness of God, his Banner, under-scored his conviction that God was alive and under-girded his praise of Jehovah. The streamers, banners, dancing, and the shouts of jubilation that accompanied the victorious march home from his battles were positive expressions of worship. David was not the hero. God was! The march became a triumphant procession in honor of the glorious Conqueror who had subdued yet another enemy.

Perhaps, when we find ourselves weary with the struggle and tired of the conflict, we should do what David did: praise *Jehovah-Nissi* until He distills as the dew upon our lives and His protection and direction become cause for rejoicing and jubilation. We may be in a battle, but we are not in charge of the army. "The battle is the LORD's" (1 Samuel 17:47).

David never lost sight of the value of praising the

name of *Jehovah-Nissi*. He said, "You are holy, enthroned in the praises of Israel." David was not seeking to manipulate God with praise, for he knew God was far too holy to be controlled by the words of mere men. He praised the name of God, for that made the nature of God available to him in time of need.

CHAPTER 7

David Worshiped a Holy God

Jehovah-M'kaddesh

Among the many explicit passages that David wrote, few are more beautiful or expressive of the way true believers feel than his cry, "The law of the LORD is perfect, converting the soul; the testimony of the LORD is sure, making wise the simple; the statutes of the LORD are right, rejoicing the heart; the commandment of the LORD is pure, enlightening the eyes; the fear of the LORD is clean, enduring forever; the judgments of the LORD are true and righteous altogether. More to be desired are they than gold, yea, than much fine gold; sweeter also than honey and the honeycomb. Moreover by them Your servant is warned, and in keeping them there is great reward" (Psalm 19:7-11).

Again and again, David and the other psalmists declare that God's Law is perfect and is the object of their love. This should be sufficient proof that David had access to copies of the first five books of the Old Testament. He was familiar with the Law, and he found it the source of much rejoicing, strength, and security.

That is not always the way New Testament believers view the Law. In my annual reading through the Bible, I find the written law threatening. I discover that I have done many of the "don't's." Also, I realize that I have not yet done many of the "do's." I can easily tremble, rather than rejoice, when I read the extreme verdicts God has given to those who disobey the Divine Law.

By the time I get near the end of Leviticus, I have convinced myself there is no chance whatsoever of my ever being holy. God set the standard for holiness beyond my reach. None of my believing, behaving or achieving will ever catapult me into the holiness of God. This realization is the stated purpose for the Law. This is why the Law was written. Paul explains it, "I would not have known sin except through the law. For I would not have known covetousness unless the law had said, 'You shall not covet' " (Romans 7:7), and "The law was our tutor to bring us to Christ, that we might be justified by faith" (Galatians 3:24). We need to remember that the Law came at the request of the Israelites, who preferred to follow commands from God rather than live in fellowship with God. God's revealed Presence on Mt. Sinai was too awesome for them — they opted for the security of clear-cut orders such as their Egyptian taskmasters had issued to them. In the pride of their new way of life, these former slaves convinced themselves they could be or do anything that God required of them. All they needed was direction. They thought that freedom from a taskmaster equated to a change of nature. Their exodus did elevate their position, but it did not change their condition in life.

How slow we are to learn that emancipation from sin

is not the same as transformation of character. The initial work of the cross breaks the power of canceled sin to set the prisoner free, but that former captive is not yet God-like. The distance between himself and His redeeming God is incomparable. To help us grasp the difference between our standing before God and our state in life, God has given us His Law. The purpose of the Law is not to make us holy, but to convince us of what David said: "There is none who does good, No, not one" (Psalm 14:3). Many generations later, Paul echoed this when he wrote, "There is none righteous, no, not one" (Romans 3:10). The LORD gave Aaron, the high priest, a specific law and said, "It shall be a statute forever throughout your generations, that you may distinguish between holy and unholy, and between unclean and clean" (Leviticus 10:9-10). Only God is holy, and the Law illuminates this like a giant spotlight.

Jehovah-M'kaddesh

Near the end of the third book of the Law, right in the midst of a series of penalties for idolatry, consulting spirits, cursing parents, and committing sexual sins, God declared, "I am the LORD who sanctifies you" (Leviticus 20:8). It is another compound or covenant name of God — Jehovah-M'kaddesh — "the LORD your holiness." Having convinced us of our total inability to be what God desires us to be, to say nothing of our failures to do what God has commanded us to do, God says: "I am your holiness. I sanctify you." What we cannot become, He already is, and He has made that nature available to us.

That David was aware of this covenant name of God is clear from his cry, "Bless the LORD, O my soul; and all that is within me, bless His *holy name*" (Psalm 103:1, emphasis added). David viewed the Law as a holy law because a holy God gave it to us. This king could delight in God's Law, for he had learned that God never requires from us what He has not made available to us. God lovingly gives to us that which He demands from us. Every demand for holiness written on the pages of the Bible is balanced in this provision — *Jehovah-M'kaddesh* — I am your holiness. David was comfortable with this.

This revelation of God, our Sanctifier, or Jehovah, our Holiness, is a divine provision for all time. It is not merely a stop-gap provision of the Law for the tribes of Israel in the wilderness. To the troubled church in Corinth, Paul wrote, "You are in Christ Jesus, who became for us wisdom from God — and righteousness and sanctification and redemption" (1 Corinthians 1:30). Jehovah in the Old Testament and Jesus in the New Testament are presented to us as the source of, not a substitute for, our holiness.

He may have been the shepherd-king whose life was less than perfect, but David had learned from this name of God how to appropriate God's holy nature into his own life. He prayed, "Bow down Your ear, O LORD, hear me; for I am poor and needy. Preserve my life, for I am holy; You are my God; save Your servant who trusts in You" (Psalm 86:1-2).

Holy in Contrast

The Psalms which are credited to David show that he viewed God as Holy in contrast to false gods and persons. David declared God to be holy in His character and holy in His conduct. David, far more than the other writers of the Psalms, had extensive opportunities to see the contrast between Jehovah and the Baals of the nations he conquered. Baal was the male god of the Phoenicians and Canaanites, and Ashtaroth was the female counterpart. The idolaters worshiped these images with flagrant sensuality, immorality, and human sacrifices. There were different names for the gods of other nations, but the form of worship was unchanged. These worshipers were taught that their gods were sensual, cruel and harsh, and needed constant expiation. The carved images were carried into battle, and any victories achieved were credited to them. The worshipers, because of their concept of their gods, became much like them. They were cruel, sensual, bloodthirsty, and very difficult to appease. It is far more than a truism: "Like god, like people" is a reality recorded repeatedly throughout history.

In extreme contrast to the groves, shrines and temples built on the hills of the pagan countries in which worshipers practiced all forms of vice in the names of their gods, David saw God's dwelling place as absolutely holy. He wrote, "I cried to the LORD with my voice, and He heard me from His holy hill" (Psalm 3:4), and on another occasion he asked, "LORD, who may abide in Your tabernacle? Who may dwell in Your holy hill?" (Psalm 15:1). In David's mind, the hill of God was a *holy hill*. The very Presence of the Almighty made it holy, and all behavior had to be holy behavior.

In his songs to the Chief Musician, David sang, "God [is] in His *holy* habitation" (Psalm 68:5), "The LORD is in His *holy* temple, the LORD'S throne is in heaven" (Psalm 11:4), and "In fear of You I will worship toward Your *holy* temple" (Psalm 138:1-2 All *italics* added). David's answer to his awareness of inward unholiness was to praise the name of his holy God until that holiness distilled around him like the dew of the morning.

Holy in Character

Every expression of petition, praise, and worship that David released to God, he communicated to a *holy* God whose dwelling place was *holy* by virtue of the divine Presence. Still, David had to admit, "O God, You are more awesome than Your holy places" (Psalm 68:35). It is the character of God that makes the habitation of God sacred.

David seemed to realize that God's name was intrinsically holy because God Himself is inherently holy. There is nothing we can do to increase the sacredness of that name, and there is nothing that man can do to decrease God's holiness. If we would ask a trained theologian to define the essential nature of God, he or she would likely declare, "The Lord our God is omnipotent, omniscient, omnipresent and eternal. Blessed be the name of the Lord." But the angels in heaven, who have never studied in our seminaries, simply proclaim, "Holy, Holy, Holy is the LORD of hosts" (Isaiah 6:3). Holiness is the essential nature of God Himself.

God is holy in contrast to everything and everyone else in existence. Theologians often say, "Holiness is otherwiseness," meaning that God is different in every way. Holiness is the difference of perfection versus imperfection. One of the difficulties both David and we have in understanding God is having nothing on earth with which to compare this holy God. He is holy; we are not. His abode is holy; ours is under a curse. The ways of God are holy ways, but the ways of men are unholy. We have no point of reference.

God *is* holy! It is not a title or an office that He fills. It is descriptive of the very being of God. David viewed the Spirit of God as absolutely Holy, for he prayed, "Do not take Your Holy Spirit from me" (Psalm 51:11). Looking forward prophetically to Christ's crucifixion and burial, he sang, "You will not leave my soul in Sheol, nor will You allow Your Holy One to see corruption" (Psalm 16:10). Peter effectively quoted this verse in his sermon on the day of Pentecost (Acts 2:31).

David saw God the Father as holy — "You are holy" (Psalm 22:3); he visualized God's Son as holy — "Holy One" (Psalm 16:10), and he recognized God's Spirit as holy — "Holy Spirit" (Psalm 51:11). God had granted David amazing prophetic insight for the day in which he lived. However limited or enlarged his vision of God was, it embraced the holy nature of that God.

Holy in Conduct

In a Psalm of praise, David exclaimed, "The LORD is righteous in all His ways, and holy in all His works" (Psalm 145:17, AV). The New King James translation says, "Gracious in all His works." While none of God's works make Him holy, the fact that He *is* holy shows up in His works — they are gracious works, or works that display His gracious nature.

In one of his Michtams, David wrote, "O my soul, you have said to the LORD, 'You are my Lord, My goodness is nothing apart from You' " (Psalm 16:2). What a magnificent proclamation of the availability of God's holiness here and now for you and me. If *Jehovah-M'kaddesh* is my holiness and my sanctification, then there is no other source for them — "My goodness is nothing apart from You."

In saying this, David recognized that holiness is not achieved; it is received. It is not likely that he understood how it worked, but he was content to have it function in his life. Theologians contend that holiness is not imputed by God, and they are probably correct. Holiness is not imputed *to* persons, it is *indwelt* in them.

Jesus explained this to His disciples when He told them, "It is to your advantage that I go away; for if I do not go away, the Helper will not come to you; but if I depart, I will send Him to you" (John 16:7). He had already defined this "Helper" as the Holy Spirit (see

John 14:26). Although Christ had been *with* them, Jesus promised that this Helper would be *in* them (see John 14:17). Jesus did go away in the ascension. On the day of Pentecost, the Father kept the promise of Jesus and sent the Holy Spirit to the waiting believers in the upper room. In contrast to the titles given by Jesus, once the Spirit arrived, He was no longer called "the Helper" or "the Spirit of Truth." The New Testament consistently calls Him the *Holy* Spirit.

This third person of the Trinity has the special title "Holy." He has the distinctive ministry of revealing God's holiness in and through the lives of believers. He dwells within, seeking to make such changes as will best demonstrate God's nature. By bearing the fruit of the Spirit and by giving guidance to individual behavior, the Holy Spirit brings the holiness of God into the daily lives of Christians. Because He lives within us, He produces the holiness — His essential nature — that has eluded us for so long.

Holiness does not come by striving, but by submitting. We do not work at being holy; we live in union with the Holy Spirit within us and holiness results. The inward work of the Spirit is called "sanctification." The outer results are called "holiness," although admittedly, both words come from the same Hebrew and Greek words. In this same song where David sang, "My goodness is nothing apart from You," he wrote a verse that says, "To the saints who are on the earth, They are the excellent ones, in whom is all my delight" (Psalm 16:3). In a day of limited revelation, David recognized that God is making us to be saints. God actually calls us saints while we are still on earth. Few have trouble acknowledging there are saints in heaven, but many find it difficult to see them in the local congregation. Sainthood here on earth does not require beautification by a religious body. True saints are a result of the work of the indwelling Spirit of God, and the Bible consistently calls the believers "saints." Paul alone calls us saints nearly forty times in his epistles.

David sensed that if we are holy by God's action, we can act holy and not be "holier-than-thou." If we have not achieved holiness by virtue of our works, we can certainly take no credit for any level of holiness that others may see in us. This should destroy all pride and sense of superiority. We may manifest God's holiness in different areas than others do, but, in turn, they may have allowed the Holy Spirit to work a transformation in areas of their lives that we have consistently resisted. The difference does not lie in inferiority or superiority. It is simply a difference.

David's behavior through his reign as king indicates that he felt he was a hypocrite if he acted any way other than holy. He knew that he had been chosen of God, set apart by God and anointed of God. This was enough to convince him that he should act harmoniously with this special work of God's grace within him. He dared to declare about himself what God had said about him, and he lived a righteous life before others.

Holiness is not a state of mind or a feeling; it is the Person of the Holy Spirit at work within us. When we are especially aware of our human nature and its unholiness, we should do what David did: praise the name of *Jehovah-M'kaddesh* — "The Lord our Holiness." We can enjoy His Presence as our holiness and sanctification if we will praise His Holy name until He distills in our lives as the refreshing dew of the morning.

David declared this, for in the Psalm of the Cross, he said, "But You are holy, Who inhabit the praises of Israel" (Psalm 22:3). The God Who descends into our midst to enjoy our times of praise and worship is Holy. As we praise Him, we create an acceptable atmosphere for the Holy God to come into our presence with His Holy nature. Who can be in His Presence without becoming a little more like Him? David certainly could not.

When David found himself in the Presence of a Holy God, there was not enough persuasion in all of the philosophers of the world to change his mind about God's being alive. He was enjoying the energizing force of God's holiness. Of course God was alive! This reinforced conviction, plus the realized nature of a Holy God, lifted David's worship to realms of ecstasy. He knew the God he worshiped, and he had a small measure of the nature of that God with which to express worship. *Jehovah-M'kaddesh* always makes worship more exact, explicit, and eloquent. As we allow Him to become our holiness, we better understand His nature. When we accept that He has set us aside and sanctified us to worship Him, we then move in divine authority. Furthermore, the more we grant the resident Holy Spirit liberty to express worship through us, the more exquisite it becomes. He knows far better than we how to magnify the Almighty.

David was far more than a poet and a talented musician. The secret of the beauty of his Psalms lies in his knowledge of God and the nature of that God shining through his songs and praise. David wrote under the inspiration of the Holy Spirit, and God's Spirit knows how to magnify and extol the godhead.

David not only found the Presence of a Holy God to be a producer of holiness within himself, but he learned that this same God can become the peace that is so needed when the responsibilities of leadership press heavily on us.

CHAPTER 8

David Worshiped God as His Peace

Jehovah-Shalom

The holiness of God is pictured throughout the Bible, but this revelation is seldom as comforting as it is distressing. The greater the distance between the nature of God and the nature of man, the more difficult relationship becomes. Usually the appearance of an angel caused Old Testament believers to expect death rather than blessing. Even the limited measure of God's holiness His heavenly messengers reflect is so much higher than man's fallen nature as to make their presence a very uncomfortable experience.

David knew this well, but he had become quite comfortable in the personal relationship with God he had developed on the hillsides while tending the sheep. It is not to be assumed, however, that the men who surrounded him were equally at peace with God. They came from very different backgrounds than David's.

While David was in the process of training his 400

volunteers to become a fighting unit whose trust was in God, it can be safely assumed that he told these men the story of Gideon, Israel's hero in the conflict with the Midianites during the days of the judges. The Scripture's account of the story begins, "Then the children of Israel did evil in the sight of the LORD. So the LORD delivered them into the hand of Midian for seven years" (Judges 6:1). Israel had known other oppression, but none as severe as this one. The Midianites and the Amalekites united to raid Israel, especially during the harvest. Using the "scorched earth" policy, they left nothing behind them. They stole what they wanted of the crops, and then they destroyed what was left, including the stubble. So many houses were demolished that the Bible records, "Because of the Midianites, the children of Israel made for themselves the dens, the caves, and the strongholds which are in the mountains" (Judges 6:2).

The prophet God sent told them this was the result of their past actions; it was their own fault. If they had completely obeyed God and destroyed the Midianites under the leadership of Joshua, there would have been no Midianite nation to captivate them. What didn't seem to be worth the effort a generation or so ago was now beyond their abilities. Half-hearted obedience to God in days past had set the scene for this present oppression. David knew well that what we will not capture in our personal lives often grows strong enough to capture us. It is a case of conquer or be conquered; rule or be ruled!

Some writers stumble at David's cruelty in battle. Repeatedly, we read of him killing all the inhabitants of a city; men, women, children, and babies. Even after capturing a portion of an army, he sometimes slaughtered them rather than keep them in captivity. It appears to be barbaric, and it certainly does not fit our modern concepts, but David's actions were the result of what he learned from Israel's earlier history. He knew that a subjugated enemy required constant watching and frequent reconquering. David merely set himself to destroy the nations that Joshua had invaded without completely annihilating the inhabitants. What David could learn from the sacred history, he did not have to learn through painful personal experience.

The God of Peace

Among those who had not yet fled to the caves in the mountains were Gideon and his family. That they were under the oppression of the Amalekites is seen in Gideon's threshing wheat in a winepress rather than on a threshing floor. While this greatly restricted this activity, it also protected the harvest from the enemy. Gideon was providing food for his family in the midst of an enemy-produced famine. His personal participation in this threshing, rather than assigning one of the servants to the task, shows the courage of the man.

While he was working in the winepress, an Angel of the LORD appeared to Gideon and said, "The LORD is with you, you mighty man of valor!" At this point in telling the story, David dramatically turned a complete circle, pretending to look for the mighty man of valor, as Gideon probably did that day.

Finding himself alone in the winepress, Gideon said, "God is with me? If He is really with me, how come we are in such distress and oppression?"

Employing a favorite tactic of God, the Angel of the LORD ignored Gideon's questions of unbelief and said, "Go in this might of yours, and you shall save Israel from the hand of the Midianites. Have I not sent you?" (Judges 6:14).

David loved to point out to his men that God is far less interested in explaining "why" than He is in declaring "what." No commander has the time, or the responsibility, to explain why certain actions are necessary in time of war. Generals give commands without explanation, and the responsibility of the troops is to obey without explanation, qualification or hesitation. Military success is dependent upon this relationship between the commander and the commanded. Implicit trust is essential on both sides. The commanded must trust the wisdom of the commander, and the commander must be able to trust the obedience of the commanded if the campaign is to be successful. David wanted this to be clearly understood before he ever led these troops into conflict with Saul. The story of Gideon helped him to make this point. God's only response to Gideon's question was, "Have I not sent you?" Nothing else mattered. This was more than enough authority for Gideon. As he later learned, Israel would recognize and respond to this authorization to rise up against the common enemy.

Once Gideon accepted this authority pattern, the Angel began to give Gideon specific instructions. They began with a challenge to tear down the wooden image of Baal on his father's property. Gideon was instructed to use the wood from that altar to offer a burned sacrifice unto the LORD on the very site where Hebrews had worshiped Baal.

Perhaps David asked his men what we so often ask ourselves when we read this passage: "Why does God so often insist that we put our homes in order before He will entrust us to deliver others from enemy oppression?" God knows that if we cannot make it work in our own lives, it is hypocrisy to try to make it work in the lives of others.

Both fearful and doubtful, Gideon wanted a sign of the authenticity of this dangerous commission. He asked the Angel to wait until he could prepare an offering. This was consistent with the custom of his day. Usually, when a prophet shared a word from the LORD to a person, the recipient responded with a gift of food for the prophet and a sacrifice for God. When Gideon returned with a young goat and a loaf of bread, "The Angel of God said to him, 'Take the meat and the unleavened bread and lay them on this rock, and pour out the broth.' And he did so. Then the Angel of the LORD put out the end of the staff that was in His hand, and touched the meat, and the unleavened bread; and fire rose out of the rock and consumed the meat and the bread. And the Angel of the LORD departed out of his sight" (Judges 6:20-21).

This was enough proof for Gideon, and, predictably, his response was to expect death. But God had not come to kill Gideon. He wanted to use him in liberating Israel. To calm his fears, "The LORD said to him, 'Peace *[shalom]* be with you; do not fear, you shall not die.' So Gideon built an altar there to the LORD, and called it *Jehovah-Shalom* — The Lord Is Peace" (Judges 6:23-24).

Jehovah was using the serious problem that Gideon was in to form the background for the revelation of still another of the compound names for God. Gideon was going to bring peace to his nation because of *Jehovah-Shalom!* God was revealing still another facet of His divine nature to His covenant people. Even when their disobedience cost them their peace, it did not affect the essential nature of God. God is Peace, regardless of our behavior, for nothing we can do can change that nature.

This declaration may have seemed premature to

David's men, for nothing in Gideon's circumstances had changed. He was still hiding in the winepress. The Midianites were still in control, and the image of Baal still stood in the family yard. It might have seemed wiser for God to have made this declaration after Gideon's victory, after he smashed Midian's might conclusively. But Gideon needed peace before the battle more than he needed it after the conflict. David wanted his men to know that a battle directed by *Jehovah-Shalom* was based on peace and security rather than on fear and anxiety, for the very nature of the Supreme Leader is Peace.

This revelation to Gideon of a new name for God would be easy for David to understand. David had repeatedly told the story of Abraham paying tithes to Melchizedek, king of Salem, after the successful conquest of the kings who had captured Sodom and Gomorrah. Lot and his family were captured in this battle. To rescue them, Abraham armed the men in his household and fought successfully against these kings. Rather than receive payment from the king of Salem, Abraham paid tithes to him. The Book of Hebrews suggests that Melchizedek was an earthly manifestation of Christ Jesus. Theologians call this a theophanic manifestation. "King of Salem," his title, means "King of peace." Long before Gideon learned that one of God's names is "God of peace," Abraham had discovered it in this manifestation of Melchizedek. God has always been *Jehovah-Shalom*, and He will always be "The LORD our Peace."

By David's day, the word *shalom* had become a common greeting. The Old Testament uses this word twenty-five times as a greeting or a farewell. To wish one *shalom* implies a blessing, while to withhold *shalom* implies a curse. *Shalom* and *shalem* are among the most important theological words in the Old Testament. *Shalom* occurs over 250 times in 213 separate verses. It refers to a condition of freedom from disturbance, whether outwardly or inwardly, but it also means "soundness," "health," and eventually came to mean "prosperity" and well-being in general.

When David asked Uriah "how Joab was doing, and how the people were doing, and how the war prospered" (2 Samuel 11:7), he was actually inquiring about their *shalom*. He wanted to know about their well-being, their health, and their relationship to their enemies, for *shalom* also means "absence of strife."

Robert Baker Girdlestone says that *shalom* "implied a bringing of some difficulty to a conclusion, a finishing off of some work, a clearing away, by payment or labour or suffering, of some charge." (*Synonyms of the Old Testament,* page 96. Reprint of 1897 edition.) What a perfect picture of our God. Through Christ Jesus, He finished the work of redemption and cleared away the charges that sin had brought against us through the payment of His own life.

It may not be by accident that the exact center of the Bible reads, "Mercy and truth have met together; righteousness and peace have kissed each other" (Psalm 85:10). God's righteousness and peace become the very center of the life of the believer whose trust is in *Jehovah-Tsidkenu* [righteousness] and *Jehovah-Shalom* [peace]. "He Himself is our peace," Paul wrote (Ephesians 2:14). Peace is far more than a concept. Peace is a condition. It reaches beyond feeling to become a fact. It remains independent of the circumstances of life and rests completely contingent upon relationship with God.

Peace with God

Gideon, who first reacted with fear and turmoil

because of the enemy, reacted next in fear because of the angelic announcement. When the Angel accepted his offering, it convinced Gideon that this message was actually from God. When faith replaced fear, Gideon experienced peace because he was entering into God's commission for his life.

God taught Gideon that peace is not the absence of conflict; it is participating in a covenant, for *shalom* is often the result of God's activity in covenant. It is as though the Angel had said, "*Jehovah-Shalom* has sent you, Gideon, therefore 'the peace of God, which surpasses all understanding, will guard your heart(s) and mind(s) through Christ Jesus' " (Philippians 4:7).

Gideon's quick response in building an altar shows that he understood he was invited to enter into a covenant of peace with God. Within twenty-four hours, he built two altars to the LORD. The first one was at the site of the winepress, where he quickly offered a sacrifice of consecration. The next night, after he had torn down the wooden image unto Baal, he built an altar to the LORD and offered one of the oxen he had used to tear down Baal as a burned sacrifice to the LORD. This was in direct obedience to the command of the Angel of the LORD.

Gideon was not making a covenant with the LORD. He was entering into an existing covenant offered by God. All he had to do was say an obedient "amen!" to all that God had said. We are not required to make peace with God. We are simply asked to accept the peace *of* God. He *is* Peace. We need only to accept Him as He is to enter into the peace of God.

When I enter into an agreement with a publisher to write a book, they draw up a contract and mail it to me for my signature. It is my option to reject portions of the contract by drawing a line through that section and initialing this action. When I am in agreement with the contract, I merely sign it. This is my "okay" or my "amen." This brings the publisher and me into an agreement, and we can have a peaceful working relationship in the writing, editing and publishing of the book.

Similarly, Gideon's sacrifices on the altars were his way of signing the contract God had proposed to him. He was saying, "I'm your man, God. Lead on; I'll follow." Peace is always the by-product of uncompromising obedience to God. The only way to have peace with God is to walk in obedience to Him.

Very likely, David pointed out to his men that Gideon said more than "amen" at these altars; he was entering into fellowship with God. It is not those who go into battle *for* God that maintain inner peace; it is those who go into conflict *with* God. It is not God's promise that brings peace; it is His Presence. David never forgot God's promise to Moses: "My Presence will go with you, and I will give you rest" (Exodus 33:14). Perpetual peace depends upon continued fellowship with God.

In the days that lay before them, the circumstances of David's men would be much like Gideon's. It proved profitable for David to remind his men-in-training that Gideon had a confrontation and a commission before he knew peace. He reminded them that Gideon's initial response to this encounter was the construction of an altar where that proclaimed peace could be experienced and expressed. David stressed that it does not require a change of circumstances to bring peace to our lives; just a confrontation with God that brings us into a covenant relationship, for God *is* our Peace far more than He gives peace. Peace is not as much a present as it is a Presence.

David probably told his men that when Phinehas, the son of Eleazar and the grandson of Aaron, demonstrated his zeal for the LORD, God gave a promise to him. It was, "Behold, I give to him My covenant of peace, and it shall be to him and his descendants after him a covenant of an everlasting priesthood" (Numbers 25:12-13).

God taught these priestly descendants of Phinehas to bless Israel by saying, "The LORD bless you and keep you; the LORD make His face shine upon you, and be gracious to you; the LORD lift up His countenance upon you, and give you peace" (Numbers 6:24-26). Those who are in a covenant of peace with God can extend God's peace to others.

Peace of God

Persons who through self-surrender have come into peace with God will consistently experience the peace of God, for the blessing of God's Presence is peace. In the oldest book in the Bible, we read, "Now acquaint yourself with Him, and be at peace; thereby good will come to you" (Job 22:21). David was familiar with this, for he wrote, "As for me, I will call upon God, and the LORD shall save me. Evening and morning and at noon I will pray, and cry aloud, and He shall hear my voice. He has redeemed my soul in peace from the battle which was against me" (Psalm 55:16-18).

David came on the scene too early to hear the prophet Isaiah declare: "For unto us a Child is born, unto us a Son is given; and the government will be upon His shoulder. And His name will be called Wonderful, Counselor, Mighty God, Everlasting Father, *Prince of Peace*" (Isaiah 9:6), or "You will keep him in perfect peace, whose mind is stayed on You, because he trusts in You" (Isaiah 26:3). An unidentified psalmist, who could have been David, said: "Great peace have those who love Your law, and nothing causes them to stumble" (Psalm 119:165).

David could not know that after the resurrection, Jesus would consistently greet His disciples with the words, "Peace to you" (John 20:26), thereby replacing their fears with His peace; but David must have understood this principle, for he sang, "The LORD will bless His people with peace" (Psalm 29:11). He knew that "The meek shall inherit the earth, and shall delight themselves in the abundance of peace" (Psalm 37:11).

Neither could David know that Paul would define the work of God's Spirit within the believer by saying, "The fruit of the Spirit is love, joy, *peace,* longsuffering, kindness, goodness, faithfulness, gentleness, self-control" (Galatians 5:22-23). But he taught his men to "Depart from evil, and do good; seek peace, and pursue it" (Psalm 34:14). David may have been an Old Testament saint, but he knew the God of both Testaments. He knew that Jehovah was a God of peace Who had made peace with God available, and Who offered the peace of God to those who would fellowship with Him.

Jehovah-Shalom was the object of David's worship, and because of this, David could sing, "Mark the blameless man, and observe the upright; for the future of that man is peace" (Psalm 37:37). David associated a close relationship with God as being the source of his peace, and this is what God was revealing to Gideon. The peace that David had found in the quietness on the hillsides was also present in the turbulence of battle. David testified that God was with him when he tended sheep and when he led the army. The peace David knew in the security of the palace was as real as when he was hiding in a cave. Circumstances neither produced nor destroyed David's peace, for it was the peace of God, and God was with him at all times.

David's knowledge of *Jehovah-Shalom* was a constant reinforcement of his conviction that God lived. While it may not be as sound theologically as a passage from the Bible, there is something to be said for the little chorus we used to sing in my religious heritage: "You ask me how I know He lives? He lives within my heart!" The inner tranquility that David experienced when everything around him was in turmoil was further evidence to Him that God was a living God Who was worthy of our worship.

One of the major disturbances to true worship is the loss of peace. When the soul is shouting in fear and anxiety, the spirit has difficulty focusing upon the Lord Jesus Christ. It is when we are at rest inwardly that we worship best. The God of Peace has brought the peace of God into our hearts by Christ Jesus, so our worship can ascend without distracting inner conflicts. We need to accept Jehovah as our *shalom*, both for our sakes and for His sake. Worship demands it.

Most Christians have experienced a measure of God's peace. When they were saved from sin, they enjoyed the peace of release. It was restful to learn that sin no longer had dominion over their lives. As they related to the work of Christ, the Reconciler of men to God, they began to experience the peace of restored relationship. The more they learned to surrender the control of their lives to the authority of the Lord, the more they enjoyed the peace of submission.

However, many Christians have discovered that peace is not necessarily permanent. Peace wears thin when it is separated from the Person Who imparted that peace. More than that, peace in circumstance "A" may not mean peace in circumstance "B". It will require the surrender of "B" to the rule of *Jehovah-Shalom* to bring it into the same peace.

We need the Presence of "The Prince of Peace" in all circumstances of life to maintain inner tranquility, trust, confidence, and calm assurance. It is in relationship that we find divine peace.

Perhaps it was easy for David to accept Jehovah as his *Shalom,* for he had long known God as his Shepherd.

CHAPTER 9

David Worshiped God as His Shepherd

Jehovah-Rohi

Except for the Lord's Prayer, more people have memorized the Twenty-Third Psalm than any other passage of Scripture. It has been a source of comfort to thousands who have walked "through the valley of the shadow of death," burying their loved ones who had died. Men and women, young and old, the learned and the unlearned all enjoy this Psalm. Its utter simplicity, much like our Lord's parables, unfolds a message of profound depths. What at first appears to be waters to wade in turns out to be waters to swim in. The very reading, or quoting, of this passage has brought peace to millions of troubled and fearful hearts.

This Psalm is often called "The Pearl of Psalms," and "The Nightingale Psalm." Charles Spurgeon said of it, "It is David's Heavenly Pastoral; a surpassing ode, which none of the daughters of music can excel. The clarion of war here gives place to the pipe of peace, and he who so lately bewailed the woes of the shepherd tunefully rehearses the joys of the flock." He added, "Of this delightful song it may be affirmed that its piety and its poetry are equal, its sweetness and its spirituality are unsurpassed." (*The Treasury of David.*)

The Twenty-Third Psalm is the work of King David. After years of shepherding sheep, and later people, David wrote, "The LORD is my shepherd" — *Jehovah-Rohi* (Psalm 23:1). The beginning of this revelation of the covenant name of God likely started in his youth while he tended his father's sheep. Its depth of understanding suggests, however, that it was not until his mature years that David penned this short and simple soliloquy of faith, confidence, and commitment.

Most of David's Psalms express vibrant faith in God, but frequently this theme shifts to complaints or prayers for deliverance. In his joyful Psalms, David enthusiastically expresses jubilant exultation to God, but in his Shepherd Psalm, we find no complaint, prayer, or even triumphant praise. This is a Psalm of contentment, submission, and relationship. It beautifully pictures the "love, joy and peace" which Paul lists as the first fruits of the Spirit to ripen in a believer's heart. It is the resultant fruit of relationship with God. The sheep do not read books about the shepherd; they live with him. Accordingly, they become partakers of His goodness and participants of His nature.

This Psalm was written by the shepherd-king in the voice of a sheep. David did not write much from his experience as a shepherd, but more from his observation of the sheep. As a shepherd, David was forced to be a wanderer. His business was to lead his sheep over vast tracts of wilderness territory, always looking for pasture and water. He carried weapons to defend the sheep when predators attacked. His life as a shepherd was solitary and lonely. His companions were the silent stars by night and the speechless sheep by day. Predictably, this formed a wonderfully close union between the shepherd and his sheep. Originally, they were far apart, as he, a man, was made in the image of God, and they were irrational animals that perish. Yet the distance between them gradually lessened. The shepherd stooped to feel the weakness and the dependence of the sheep, and he came to know them, even giving each of them a name. When he called them, they followed him.

Jesus seemed to love this image, for He often spoke of Himself as the Shepherd of His sheep. He left His heavenly abode and "became flesh and dwelt among us" (John 1:14). He learned to "sympathize with our weaknesses" (Hebrews 4:15), and "He can have compassion on those who are ignorant and going astray" (Hebrews 5:2). "He calls his own sheep by name and leads them out. And when he brings out his own sheep, he goes before them; and the sheep follow him, for they know his voice" (John 10:3-4). Little wonder, then, that Jesus said, "I am the good shepherd; and I know My sheep, and am known by My own" (John 10:14).

This remarkable union was produced by the condescension — the stooping down — of the shepherd and the unquestioning trust on the part of the sheep. The sheep could never rise to the level of the shepherd, no matter how well they matured, but the shepherd could lower himself to the level of the sheep. This condescending love of the shepherd produces an ascending love in the sheep which allows them to find a level for fellowship.

There is no more beautiful sound in all the music of the Bible than *Jehovah-Rohi* — "the LORD is my shepherd." Isaiah saw this and wrote, "He will feed His flock like a shepherd; He will gather the lambs with His arm, and carry them in His bosom, and gently lead those who are with young" (Isaiah 40:11). David, well experienced in shepherding, wrote "The LORD is *my* shepherd." The emphasis is upon the possessive pronoun "my." God is not pictured as a beekeeper whose love is for the hive and the honey, and who would have little, if any, concern over individual bees — much less calling them by name. He is characterized as a Shepherd Who has intimate knowledge of every sheep in the flock. David felt the comfort of individual care in the midst of the flock.

As a young shepherd of sheep, David was restless and filled with confidence in himself. He bragged to King Saul that he had single-handedly killed a lion and a bear. As an older shepherd of people, after a long-term kingship over all of Israel, David wrote and sang of the security of sheep whose shepherd was perfect in all of His care for them. Like most of us, it was only after grievous falls, long repentance, and a daily growing conviction of God's forgiveness and continued protection that David could settle down to such perfect rest. Lambs enjoy all the benefits of being shepherded without ever relating to the shepherd, but the mature sheep in the flock come to recognize that everything they enjoy comes as a provision of their shepherd.

There is nothing in this Psalm that extols the sheep. Everything stated eulogizes the Shepherd. All provision is His provision. The enjoyed protection is because of the Shepherd's rod and staff. Even the peace that the sheep experience is because the Shepherd accepts responsibility for every need the sheep will ever experience. How comforting, then, to acknowledge *Jehovah-Rohi,* "The LORD is my Shepherd."

Lambs may believe they belong to themselves, but

there comes a time when they recognize that the
shepherd owns them completely. When he shears
them, the wool is his. If he sells them, the money is his,
and if he should choose to slaughter them, the meat
belongs to him. The sheep of the flock are the property
of the shepherd. He purchased them, and no one but
himself has any right to the flock. Paul recognized this,
for he wrote, "Do you not know that your body is the
temple of the Holy Spirit who is in you, whom you have
from God, and you are not your own? For you were
bought at a price; therefore glorify God in your body
and in your spirit, which is God's" (1 Corinthians
6:19-20).

Many years ago, a missionary spoke at the church I
was pastoring. During his services, he introduced a
simple chorus that went: "I'm not my own; I'm Yours.
I'm not my own; I'm Yours. Bought with the blood of
Jesus, I'm not my own; I'm Yours." Then he had us
sing it in the voice of the Spirit: "You're not your own;
you're mine." My congregation and I had considerable
difficulty singing this song with any depth of meaning.
I had always known this truth intellectually, but this
song was a confession that called for an experiential
expression. When I finally made that full consecration,
I stood with arms upraised and sang the chorus with
tears running down my face.

It is impossible to meaningfully say "The LORD is
my shepherd" without fully acknowledging that He
therefore has complete ownership of all that we are, all
that we have, and all that we will ever be. We would not
exist except for the action of the flock that brought us
forth as lambs. Everything that He does for us is
because we are His. In providing for us, and in protecting us, He is preserving His own property. As the
psalmist put it, "So we, Your people and sheep of Your
pasture, will give You thanks forever" (Psalm 79:13).

Like the love-slave who, when his time of service had ended, chose to remain under the protective care of his master, we too have entered into a lifetime relationship with our Jehovah-Shepherd. We have gone to the doorpost and allowed the Master to pierce our earlobes with an awl and to place a golden earring in the hole. This declares to everyone that we do not belong to ourselves, but we belong to the One to Whom we have chosen to submit the care of our lives.

This is not one-sided, however. Not only are we His sheep, but "The LORD is my Shepherd. He owns me as a sheep, but I own Him as my Shepherd." As the Shulamite maiden proclaimed, "My beloved is mine, and I am his. He feeds his flock among the lilies" (Song of Solomon 2:16).

Obligation of Sheep and Shepherd

Jehovah-Rohi accepts His sheep as more than chattel. He enters into a covenant relationship with them. They "shall not want" as long as they remain in this relationship. At whatever point they seek pastures for themselves, they may perish for lack of food and water, or they may become prey to the wolves and the bears. However, if they genuinely submit to "The LORD ... my shepherd," these concerns never become theirs.

The obvious responsibility of the shepherd is provision and protection. The Good Shepherd leads and feeds His sheep. He gives rest and refreshment to them. He determines their movements and their times of rest. "No good thing will He withhold from those who walk uprightly" (Psalm 84:11). Furthermore, His protection is so great that the sheep can honestly say, "Yea, though I walk through the valley of the shadow of death, I will fear no evil; for You are with me; Your rod and Your staff, they comfort me" (Psalm 23:4). The fearful unknown to the sheep is familiar territory to the shepherd, so the sheep merely trust what the shepherd knows. The forceful enemies of the sheep become the foes of the shepherd, and he soon drives off or destroys them. That is his job — his obligation.

Of course, there is equally an obligation of the sheep to the shepherd. Their first responsibility is to follow the shepherd. Eastern shepherds do not drive their sheep or use sheep dogs to herd them. The movement of the flock depends upon the sheep's willingness to follow the shepherd anywhere he leads. As we all know, the best leader is only of value if he is followed.

Most sheep are willing to follow the shepherd out of the rock pile into the green pastures with the cool, flowing waters. This ample supply seems so permanent that the sheep never consider that some morning the shepherd will clap his hands, calling the sheep to follow him to a higher pasture range. Few sheep take this action seriously, and they refuse to move. A few of the malcontents and the mentally deranged finally follow the shepherd (at least, that is what the rest of the flock call them). Those who remain elect a lead sheep as their shepherd, and they organize the pasture and set up fences to keep other sheep out.

Soon, however, these sheep learn what the shepherd knew all along: a change of season is upon them. The rains cease, the fields dry up, and the water stops flowing. This is when these sheep organize intercessory groups to plead with God to "send the rains, Lord! You've done it before, and You can do it again." They just don't realize that God seldom repeats Himself. His provision is not to renew what has become depleted, but to lead them into that which is fresh and new. He has provided a Shepherd to lead the flock into fresh pastures, but if they won't follow Him, there is no other provision for them.

All over the world, you can find the bleaching bones of Christian sheep who refused to follow Christ into new pastures. They remained with the old and starved to death. They left great memorials to past blessings, but they did not preserve life for coming generations. Sheep, and Christians, should follow the Shepherd without explanation, reservation, or hesitation. Only then dare they testify, "I shall not want."

Sheep do not take a vote to determine if the shepherd's guidance is correct. Having yielded their lives to His leadership, whether they think it is right or wrong, they must follow or perish. How we Christians need to walk in this commitment to our Shepherd. He doesn't have to explain "why." He merely leads us into His way, and we are required to follow Him. His guidance has always proven to be best in the past, so we dare to believe that it will be right for us in the future.

Sheep are also obligated to feed and drink in the pastures the shepherd provides. The shepherd can lead them to the green pastures, but only the sheep can actually eat the grass. From his leadership, both of sheep and people, David must have experienced the frustration of providing what was rejected. The Great Shepherd regularly leads His sheep into pastures where they merely stand and gaze rather than stoop and graze. They buy hand-crafted leather Bibles, but they never read them. They are placed beside the still waters of the Holy Spirit, but they never drink. They talk much about the beauties of their surroundings, but they never become partakers.

When my daughters were small, finances were tight, so taking them to a restaurant was a very special treat. How frustrating it was to have them be so excited from

looking at the other diners and examining the decor
that they could not eat the meal that had been provided.
Surroundings may be exciting, but they are not nutri-
tious. As Henry Drummond once wrote: "You can't
live on air. You can't live on one another. You can't live
on what I say; but you can live on the Bread of Life,
which is Jesus Christ." (*The Life of Henry Drummond*,
p. 493.)

No matter how mature a sheep may be, it can never
become a shepherd, and no matter how developed a
Christian may become, he can never become the lord
of his life. Christ is LORD; we are not. We are not being
trained to replace Christ, we are being shepherded so
we may become mature sheep. Submission to the
Shepherd will always be a prerequisite for the sheep.
We must always follow, feed, drink, and rest at His
bidding and in the locations of His choosing. When this
becomes a settled way of life with us, we enter into an
entirely new way of life — a life that is so ordered for us
that there is no room for anxiety, worry, or fear.
Jehovah-Rohi, "The LORD is my shepherd."

There is still a further responsibility of the sheep to
the Shepherd. As the Shepherd accepts the responsibility of provision for us, we have a responsibility of
producing for Him. Each season should have a new
crop of wool, and lambs should come forth every
spring. It is this increase that becomes the reward for
the Shepherd. "The Chief Shepherd," as Peter called
Christ Jesus (1 Peter 5:4), once told His disciples, "You
did not choose Me, but I chose you and appointed you
that you should go and bear fruit, and that your fruit
should remain" (John 15:16). Sheep are chosen for
their ability to bear wool and to produce lambs. Our
Shepherd has the right to expect this of us. In the East,
the sheep were the wealth and possession of the

shepherd; the shepherd lived off his flock, and they were his inheritance. David knew this well by experience, and he wrote, "Save Your people, and bless Your inheritance; shepherd them also, and bear them up forever" (Psalm 28:9). We need to be aware that the barren sheep are the first to become lamb chops.

Opportunities for the Sheep

Complete submission to the shepherd is not limiting; it is expanding. Since all concern for provision and protection rests with the shepherd, the sheep are free to learn to relax and live. What the sheep must learn is to live the life of a sheep and not try to live the life of a shepherd. We are people, not gods. By the shepherd's guidance, the sheep learn when and where to feed. He has gone through the pasture the preceding day and removed all poisonous weeds, placing them on a rock too high to reach. This is the "table before me in the presence of my enemies" (Psalm 23:5). Everything that would harm the sheep has been put out of their reach. This safely releases the sheep from the need to constantly ascertain what is good and what is harmful.

The shepherd also imposes a time of rest. "He makes me to lie down in green pastures" (Psalm 23:2). The sheep do not need to overeat today in fear of famine tomorrow. The shepherd's provision is consistent from day to day. Furthermore, the shepherd wants to create a quiet atmosphere where the sheep can chew their cud. It is this second chewing of the food that releases the nutrients of the grass into the systems of the sheep.

The Good Shepherd brings His sheep to restful places where He hopes they will meditate, cogitate — ruminate. Fodder, hastily taken from sermons, tapes, books and even the Bible, needs to be recalled, reviewed, and renewed. It is this second ingesting of truth that makes it vital to the believer's life.

How difficult it is for Christians in this generation to come to a place of rest. Much of our failure to respond to spiritual realities is due to our fussy obsession with merely external things. Our struggle for existence, and even our struggle for amusement, serve only to imprison ourselves further in the lower elements of life. In our struggle to own things, we never possess ourselves. Only in quietness, which is essential to spiritual receptivity, do men learn the true secret of life. Great souls have always found their inspiration in quietness. Isaiah knew this long before we were born, for he wrote, "Thus says the Lord God, the Holy One of Israel: 'In returning and rest you shall be saved; in quietness and confidence shall be your strength' " (Isaiah 30:15).

This opportunity to live includes the divine provision of healing, for "You anoint my head with oil" (Psalm 23:4), David declared. The wounds, cuts, and scrapes of the day are soothed and brought into a healing process by the Shepherd's oil. God has never promised that life would be without its wounds, but He has promised His sheep the healing oil from His hand and full restoration of their souls.

Sheep who learn to leave the worries of life with the Shepherd soon discover that they can live abundantly under the care of His hand. "My cup runs over" (Psalm 23:5) is their testimony. When the Good Shepherd was here on the earth, He said of Himself, "I have come that they may have life, and that they may have it more abundantly" (John 10:10).

Sheep under Christ's care have the opportunity to live a relaxed, abundant life here on earth in fellowship both with the Shepherd and with other sheep. They are also promised eternal life, for "Surely goodness and mercy shall follow me all the days of my life; and I will dwell in the house of the LORD forever" (Psalm 23:6).

David loved this concept of *Jehovah-Rohi*, for just as he sought to make the life of the sheep as enjoyable as possible, he viewed God as desiring the same things for him. He wrote, "You will show me the path of life; in Your Presence is fullness of joy; at Your right hand are pleasures forevermore" (Psalm 16:11). How very different are these pleasures than the ones the devil tempts us into. God's pleasures exhilarate, while satan's pleasures intoxicate. The first lifts us up, while the second tears us down.

What a blessed revelation of a covenant that God has made with His people, and He guarantees it by His very nature: *Jehovah-Rohi!* David loved it and lived in it. It was the merciful gift of a God Who was alive. The shepherding care of Jehovah became the foundation for David's worship, but it was not the only stone in that foundation, for David also came to know God as *Jehovah-Tsidkenu.*

CHAPTER 10

David Worshiped God as His Righteousness

Jehovah-Tsidkenu

In David's beautiful analogy of God being his Shepherd, he stated, "He leads me in the paths of righteousness for His name's sake" (Psalm 23:3), thereby connecting righteousness with the nature of God — "For His name's sake." The statement is so simple that it is often overlooked, and yet it is so profound that it takes the help of the Holy Spirit to comprehend its vastness.

Again and again, we find this characteristic in David's writings. On the surface is simplicity, but beneath that exterior is amazing complexity. One might wonder how this shepherd-king could have such a depth of knowledge about God when he had so little of the Bible available to him. He was not a graduate of a theological seminary, nor did he have access to the many libraries available to us today. By today's standards of education, he was a self-made man with a very limited formal education, but he knew God.

Repeatedly, David inquired of the LORD both through the prophets and the priests, and he consistently talked to God directly. His Psalms are filled with his communications with God. He testified, "As for me, I will call upon God, and the LORD shall save me. Evening and morning and at noon I will pray, and cry aloud, and He shall hear my voice" (Psalm 55:16-17). Something wonderful happens when a person talks to God; God listens, and He talks back. As David communicated with God and worshiped Him, he found himself in a learning experience. Lifted into God's Presence, he spoke God's words, saw with His eyes, and felt with His heart. David came to know what God knew, not only because of this intimate communion he enjoyed with God, but he began to know God Himself. God is a self-revealing God Who yearns for us to know Him. This knowledge comes from fellowship with God through the Spirit. Paul said, "The natural man does not receive the things of the Spirit of God, for they are foolishness to him; nor can he know them, because they are spiritually discerned" (1 Corinthians 2:14).

David was far less dependent than we are upon what God had revealed to others. He wrote what God had revealed to him personally. Out of worship came revelation and an understanding of God that could never be learned from books and sermons. David got his information directly from the source — God. This is why his Psalms have simplicity and profundity in them, and it makes the Psalms beloved of both the learned and the unlearned. No matter what level in God a person may have achieved, he or she will find satisfaction and fulfillment in reading the Psalms of David.

It was because of this endless source of divine knowledge that David could write the simple statement:

"He leads me in the paths of righteousness for His name's sake" (Psalm 23:3). In this simple sentence, David extols a righteous God, His righteous paths, and His righteous purpose.

A Righteous God

David's emphasis upon the personal pronoun "He" shows that God, the Leader, is Himself righteous, or else He would not know how to lead us into righteousness. The surrounding nations did not view their idol gods as righteous. Neither were the devotees concerned with uprightness in their worshiping. In stark contrast to the perceived nature of heathen gods, "the righteous God" (Psalm 7:9) of Israel, Jehovah, leads His people righteously and leads them into His righteousness. David consistently viewed this as a positive action. He declared, "My mouth shall sing aloud of Your righteousness" (Psalm 51:14), and, "My tongue shall speak of Your righteousness and of Your praise all the day long" (Psalm 35:28). God's righteousness was an obvious cause for David's rejoicing.

God's righteousness and His holiness are interconnected. The Bible declares Jehovah to be both holy and righteous. Perhaps we could see the holiness of God as a part of His inherent nature, while the righteousness of God is the demonstration or manifestation of that holy nature in His relationship with His people. The Hebrew word for righteousness is *tsaddik*, which means "just or innocent." When David speaks of the righteousness of God, he usually refers to the absolute, uncompromising justice of God, through which His plans, promises and purposes are executed without deviation or partiality. God's righteousness assures us of divine consistency. Because God was just, David could always count on Him to function according to His own laws and rules.

David did not view God as an autocratic Being Who was ruled by emotion or changed by flattery. He had met "a just God and a Savior" (Isaiah 45:21) of Whom Isaiah further testified, "The LORD of hosts shall be exalted in judgment, and God who is holy shall be hallowed in righteousness" (Isaiah 5:16).

In the final song of Moses, he sang, "He is the Rock, His work is perfect; for all His ways are justice, a God of truth and without injustice; righteous and upright is He" (Deuteronomy 32:4). This would certainly have been in the repertoire of David's music, for the reason Moses wrote the song was to give Israel a musical remembrance of God and His ways with people. David said almost the same thing when he wrote, "The LORD is righteous in all His ways, gracious in all His works" (Psalm 145:17).

That God is righteous is a declaration of Scripture that is not open for debate. He is upright in all of His relationships, honest in all of His dealings, and faithful in all of His promises. He is unvarying in His nature, immovable in His attitude, and unchanging in His action. His thoughts toward us are pure, His purposes are permanent, and His love is constant. His righteousness is never subject to situation ethics. "Righteous are You, O LORD, and upright are Your judgments. Your testimonies, which You have commanded, are righteous and very faithful" (Psalm 119:137-138), the psalmist wrote. One would expect David to sing this theme in a major key with full instrumentation.

This righteous nature of God was a constant source of rejoicing for David. He instructed the Chief Musician to sing to the accompaniment of stringed instruments, "Let the peoples praise You, O God; let all the peoples praise You. Oh, let the nations be glad and sing for joy! For You shall judge the people righteously, and govern the nations on earth. Selah" (Psalm 67:3-4). On another occasion David wrote, "Let the heavens rejoice, and let the earth be glad; let the sea roar, and all its fullness; let the field be joyful, and all that is in it. Then all the trees of the woods will rejoice before the LORD. For He is coming, for He is coming to judge the earth. He shall judge the world with righteousness, and the peoples with His truth" (Psalm 96:11-13). David's joy was not merely that God would judge the world, but that He would execute righteous judgment with all the peoples of the earth. The constancy of God's nature was what delighted David, for he recognized that God would act in equity, justice, and faithfulness, because God is righteous by nature.

Righteous Path

David knew that any paths God would lead him into would be righteous paths because of God's righteous nature. His use of the word *path* is his poetic expression for a way of life. He had said, "Teach me Your way, O LORD, and lead me in a smooth path, because of my enemies" (Psalm 27:11), and, "You will show me the path of life; in Your Presence is fullness of joy; at Your right hand are pleasures forevermore" (Psalm 16:11). The Good Shepherd will lead us into a way of life that involves integrity, honesty, and faithfulness — righteousness. This is, of course, consistent with the Pauline teaching of the New Testament. He told his spiritual son Titus, "The grace of God that brings salvation has appeared to all men, teaching us that, denying ungodliness and worldly lusts, we should live soberly, righteously, and godly in the present age" (Titus 2:12).

These "paths of righteousness" that our "righteous God" chooses to lead us into run north, south, east, and west in our lives. One path deals with upright living in

relationship to God, and the other path involves righteous behavior in our day-to-day dealings with one
another. Divine righteousness will involve a right
relationship with God, and it will produce a just
relationship with people, but self-righteousness offers
only a sham pretense of uprightness either with God or
man.

Righteousness between us and God will also produce
righteousness with one another, for righteousness has
both a vertical and a horizontal flow. The two lines
intercept, forming a cross in our lives. Unless both
beams of this cross are seen in a person, he or she will
not be viewed as a righteous person in the sight of God.
King Saul saw this in the life of David. After David had
mercifully spared Saul's life when he entered David's
cave, the king said to David: " 'You are more righteous
than I; for you have rewarded me with good, whereas I
have rewarded you with evil' " (1 Samuel 24:17).

David dealt righteously with Saul, but he also dealt
righteously with God, for he could honestly write,
"The LORD rewarded me according to my righteousness; according to the cleanness of my hands He has
recompensed me. For I have kept the ways of the
LORD, and have not wickedly departed from my God.
For all His judgments were before me, and I did not put
away His statutes from me. I was also blameless before
Him, and I kept myself from my iniquity. Therefore
the LORD has recompensed me according to my
righteousness, according to the cleanness of my hands
in His sight" (Psalm 18:20-24).

David learned that God does not drive us into
righteous paths; He leads us into them. Neither does
the Good Shepherd carry us on the paths of righteousness; we walk in them standing erect with our shoulders
squared. "He leadeth me" leaves a free choice for us,

for righteousness is more in behavior than in belief. It is the action of the life expressing the attitude of the heart. Progression in righteousness is the result of walking rather than talking. The lips may say righteous platitudes, but God is looking for upright lives. Being led into righteousness shows that righteousness is learned more by doing than by studying.

Since the Hebrew word used for righteousness means "just or innocent," the prophets used it to describe the person who conformed to a standard. The person was righteous because he or she lived undeviatingly according to predetermined rules. We need to be led into righteous paths, for we are incapable of either compiling those rules or conforming to them.

In the Bible's genealogy of Noah, the first thing we read is: "Noah was a just man" (Genesis 6:9). The Hebrew word that is translated here as "just" is *tsaddik*. This word is more commonly translated "righteousness." Noah dared to conform to God's standard in a time of depravity, debauchery, and departure from God, and God declared him to be a just man.

Noah lived in a time where the sinful line of Cain overshadowed the godly line of Seth. Sin, which is the exercise of self-will against the known will of God, always erodes righteousness. The Bible singles out the days of Noah as positive proof that sin disintegrates. Yet, although righteousness was very unpopular in his time, by an act of his will Noah conformed to the known will of God, and God declared him a righteous man. Believers should not concern themselves too much with the standards of the societies in which they live. God has a standard for His people, and to live according to that standard is the route to righteousness. Since God has established the criterion for righteousness — both in relationship to Himself and to others — He is best qualified to lead us into and through these paths of righteousness.

Righteous Purposes

David not only assured us that "He leadeth me in the paths of righteousness," but he gave us the reason for this — "for His name's sake" (Psalm 23:3). Good parents take the time to train their children in proper behavior and manners so they will embarrass neither the parents nor themselves. Similarly, God, Who has acknowledged us as His children by putting His name upon us, wants to teach us to "live godly in Christ Jesus" (2 Timothy 3:12). This begins with a powerful example, for children are far more apt to do what they see their parents do than to do what they say. Our Father, Who instructs us in righteous behavior, is Himself a righteous God. He leads us in paths that He walks with His children. His first line of teaching is "do what I do." David proved to be a good observer and a good learner.

David wanted continuity for his kingdom. He knew well that "God is with the generation of the righteous" (Psalm 14:5). Paul testified of David in his sermon at Antioch, "David ... served his own generation by the will of God" (Acts 13:36), but this godly king wanted to do something outstanding enough to cause people of generations to come to worship Jehovah with the love that he experienced. He proposed to build a Temple unto God, but God told him, through Nathan the prophet, that this would be unacceptable to God because of the great bloodshed for which David had been responsible. But God added, "Your house and your kingdom shall be established forever before you. Your throne shall be established forever" (2 Samuel 7:16).

Many generations later, another prophet, this time

one who was in prison because of his proclaimed message, heard God say, "For thus says the LORD: "David shall never lack a man to sit on the throne of the house of Israel' " (Jeremiah 33:17). While this is divine confirmation, it is also completion; for Jeremiah, in the final words of the preceding verse, had just declared: "THE LORD OUR RIGHTEOUSNESS" — *Jehovah-Tsidkenu* (Jeremiah 33:16).

The context of this message is gloomy. Many Hebrews had already been carried into Babylon, and now the army of Nebuchadnezzar had an impenetrable siege against Jerusalem. Jeremiah had repeatedly prophesied that the city would fall to these Chaldeans. God continued to remind the remaining citizens of their sins and iniquities. He reviewed how they had violated their covenants with the True and Living God when they began worshiping the false gods of the nations around them. In this portion of Jeremiah's prophecy, God reaffirmed His covenant with them and assured them that no amount of unrighteousness on their part could change His righteous relationship with them. He declared that His name was *Jehovah-Tsidkenu;* "The LORD of RIGHTEOUSNESS."

There comes a time in every one of our lives when our righteousness fails us. Human frailty and often personal rebellion turns our hearts away from God's paths to walk our own way, but that is not the end for any of us. Jehovah *is* our Righteousness. We may fail, but He cannot. We may sin, but He has become our Savior.

It is an inviolate principle of Scripture that what God demands from us in one place, He offers to us in another portion of the Bible. God does demand righteousness of us. David knew this intuitively, but God knows we cannot produce the righteousness that He

demands. Before Jeremiah's day, an anointed prophet
had said, "We are all like an unclean thing, and all our
righteousnesses are like filthy rags" (Isaiah 64:6). This
is as true in our day as it was in his. This defiled self-
righteousness, of course, is totally unacceptable to God,
so He became our righteousness.

David seemed to understand this, for he wrote,
"Hear me when I call, O God of my righteousness!"
(Psalm 4:1). God, Who desires to lead us into paths of
righteousness for the sake of His own name, has
willingly become the source of our righteousness. Paul
experientially declared: "You are in Christ Jesus, who
became for us wisdom from God — and righteousness
and sanctification and redemption — that, as it is
written, 'He who glories, let him glory in the LORD' "
(1 Corinthians 1:30-31).

Jehovah-Tsidkenu has become our uprightness
before God and man, "for His name's sake." All
glorying must be in the LORD, for He is the source of
our right standing before God. By His action, we have
been justified and declared righteous in His sight. As
David pled, "Oh, continue Your lovingkindness to
those who know You, and Your righteousness to the
upright in heart" (Psalm 36:10).

This righteousness of Christ that is conferred upon
those who know and love God is progressive, not
perfect. God brings us into one realm of righteousness
at a time. We mature in righteousness toward God and
toward one another. God declares us righteous; we
never deserve it. Nothing we can ever do will become
divine righteousness, but God has declared us righteous
even while we are in the process of becoming upright
in our walk before others. Furthermore, we are made
righteous from the divine viewpoint rather than the
human. Long after God declares His loving children to

be righteous, there are observers who dispute God's claim; but if God says that we are righteous, we are! What we have came as a gift. It is conferred and is not inherent, but we can learn to live in this new realm of righteousness in Christ Jesus, for He is *Jehovah-Tsidkenu.*

As his Psalms indicate, when David found himself in gross unrighteousness, he praised the LORD, his righteousness. He cooled his spirit to the dew-point until the righteous God distilled upon him as the dew of the morning. David sinned, but he refused to live as a sinner. He had learned how to secure the righteousness of God through praise. He knew what we must learn. It is one thing to fail and still another thing to live in failure. Through praise and worship of *Jehovah-Tsidkenu,* David had learned to live victoriously, uprightly, and righteously both before God and before his fellow beings.

This loving gift of righteousness from the hand of a righteous God reassured David that God was, indeed, a living God. He found God to be less exacting than He was giving. Although Jehovah demanded that His people observe a standard of behavior that conformed to the righteous Law of God, the giver of the Law was *Jehovah-Tsidkenu,* Who graciously shared his inherent righteousness with His worshipers.

It is rare for any of us to approach worship without introspectively remembering unrighteous behavior. Our consciences may remind us of yelling at our husband or wife, or slamming the door, or discourteous driving on the highway. This didn't bother us much until we began to approach the Righteous God. His Presence acts like a full-length mirror that allows us to see our unrighteous imperfections in all their hideous reality. Usually this awareness causes us to withdraw from worship, feeling that we are too unworthy to worship such a righteous God.

God has never revealed any aspect of His nature to hinder our worship. He wants us to know that He is available to us as He actually is. When we are made aware of our unrighteousness, He invites us to approach the Throne of Grace in His righteousness.

When we cannot come to God *in* righteousness, we should come to Him *for* righteousness. He is a living God easily moved by our inadequacies. Everything we need to approach Him in worship has been made available in Him.

David did not need to survive in his failure until God came on the scene, for he had come to worship an omnipresent God. He was introduced to *Jehovah-Shammah.*

CHAPTER 11

David Worshiped an Omnipresent God

Jehovah-Shammah

There is something wonderful about a faith that can embrace God as completely righteous, just, and upright and still maintain a sense of closeness with God. David had such a faith. No matter how his vision of God enlarged, he did not let it separate him from Jehovah. Perhaps it is because, like a child, he had known the closeness of God before he understood the character of God. Once a love relationship has been formed, the unveiling of the nature of the persons in that relationship brings them closer to each other rather than separating them. David had loved God before he really knew Him, and no amount of revelation was going to separate him from his God.

To say that David loved God before he really knew Him should not seem unusual. David loved and kept God's Law. The very heart of that Law was: "Hear, O Israel: The LORD our God, the LORD is one! You shall

love the LORD your God with all your heart, with all
your soul, and with all your might" (Deuteronomy
6:4-5). At least ten times, this one book of the Law
commands Israel to love the LORD. David, who had
been instructed in the Law from his boyhood up, had
responded to this commandment and loved the LORD
out of obedience and respect.

Very likely, during his youthful days when he was
tending his father's sheep, he looked up into the
heavens, or around him at the ever-changing landscape,
and sang: "The works of the LORD are great, studied by
all who have pleasure in them. His work is honorable
and glorious, and His righteousness endures forever.
He has made His wonderful works to be remembered
... He has declared to His people the power of His works
... The works of His hands are verity and justice ... Holy
and awesome is His name" (Psalm 111:2-4; 6,7,9).
Possibly the chorus to that song was, "The earth is the
LORD'S, and all its fullness, the world and those who
dwell therein" (Psalm 24:1).

When David was fleeing from Saul and hiding in
caves or in the wilderness, he could say to God, "I
remember the days of old; I meditate on all Your
works; I muse on the work of Your hands. I spread out
my hands to You; my soul longs for You like a thirsty
land. Selah" (Psalm 143:5-6).

Since we cannot love the totally unknown, God has
chosen to reveal something about Himself in His
creation. David wrote: "The heavens declare the glory
of God; and the firmament shows His handiwork. Day
unto day utters speech, and night unto night reveals
knowledge. There is no speech nor language where
their voice is not heard" (Psalm 19:1-3). David's love for
God was first sparked by observing God's handiwork,
and this is still one of the favorite tools God uses to

create an awareness of Himself. Theologians call this "revelation by design." Every watch proves the existence of a watchmaker. Similarly, if there is a world, it, too, demands a Creator.

God Knew David

Long before David really knew the LORD, Jehovah knew everything there was to know about David. He admitted, "My frame was not hidden from You, when I was made in secret, and skillfully wrought in the lowest part of the earth. Your eyes saw my substance, being yet unformed. And in Your book they all were written, the days fashioned for me, when as yet there were none of them" (Psalm 139:15-16). God's knowledge of David extended from the womb to the tomb.

David had come to realize that God fully knew and understood this king of Israel. He wrote: "O LORD, You have searched me and known me. You know my sitting down and my rising up; You understand my thought afar off. You comprehend my path and my lying down, and are acquainted with all my ways. For there is not a word on my tongue, but behold, O LORD, You know it altogether ... Such knowledge is too wonderful for me; it is high, I cannot attain it" (Psalm 139:1-4;6). In less poetic terms, David was saying, "God, You've really got my number!"

David cried, "O LORD, You have searched me and known me" (Psalm 139:1). God observed and tested this man. He knew everything he did, and He understood everything David thought (see verses 2-3). There was absolutely nothing about David that was unknown to God. He admitted, "You comprehend my path and my lying down, and are acquainted with all my ways" (verse 3). This was wonderful and awesome to David, but it did not seem to induce terror or fear. Quite the contrary, for at the end of the Psalm, David admits that God knows him better than he knows himself. He asks, "Search me, O God, and know my heart; try me, and know my anxieties; and see if there is any wicked way in me, and lead me in the way everlasting" (verses 23-24).

God Enveloped David

David did not attribute this infinite knowledge of God as much to God's omniscience as to His omnipresence. David reasoned that since God was everywhere present at all times (omnipresent), He obviously knew everything about David.

David found comfort and security in knowing God was always everywhere. When he looked at his capital city, "The city of the great King," he knew "God is in her palaces" (Psalm 48:2-3).

After admitting that God knew him far better than he knew God, David asked: "Where can I go from Your Spirit? Or where can I flee from Your Presence? If I ascend into heaven, You are there; If I make my bed in hell, behold, You are there. If I take the wings of the morning, And dwell in the uttermost parts of the sea, Even there Your hand shall lead me, and Your right hand shall hold me. If I say, 'Surely the darkness shall fall on me,' Even the night shall be light about me; Indeed, the darkness shall not hide from You, But the night shines as the day; The darkness and the light are both alike to You" (Psalm 139:7-12).

David visualized himself as totally surrounded by God day and night. He would never ascend high enough or descend deep enough to escape the Presence of God. He had found Him in the night seasons, and he had worshiped Jehovah in the heat of the day. While hiding from his enemies, David discovered the Presence of God. When sitting on the throne, David knew that he was still in the Presence of the King of kings and the LORD of lords.

David didn't view this as surveillance; he saw it as companionship and protection. He did not dread this encompassing Presence; he delighted in it. Much as a child is far more comfortable when the father is near, David found security in the omnipresence of Jehovah.

David could not think of any place he could go to escape from the Presence of the LORD. David agreed with Paul, who quoted to the Greeks from one of their own poets, "In Him we live and move and have our being" (Acts 17:28). This was a source of great comfort to David. He was never on his own, so there was never an honest reason for being lonesome. When problems of state faced David, he recognized that he need not make decisions on his own, for God was above him, beneath him, totally around him, and actually within him. Responsibilities that could have destroyed a lesser person were shared by David with the ever-present God. He wrote, "To You, O LORD, I lift up my soul ... Show me Your ways, O Lord; teach me Your paths. Lead me in Your truth and teach me, for You are the God of my salvation; on You I wait all the day" (Psalm 25:1; 4-5).

That God answered this cry is evident from David's words, "The king shall have joy in Your strength, O LORD ... You have given him his heart's desire, and have not withheld the request of his lips. Selah. For You meet him with the blessings of goodness; You set a crown of pure gold upon his head. He asked life from You, and You gave it to him ... You have made him most blessed forever; You have made him exceedingly glad with Your Presence. For the king trusts in the Lord, and through the mercy of the Most High he shall not be moved" (Psalm 21:1-4; 6-7). Such are the accrual blessings of being encompassed by God.

God was with David

In this Psalm, where David speaks so dramatically about God's enveloping Presence, David twice declared, "You are there" (Psalm 139:8), and both times he uses the Hebrew word *shammah.* Many years after David made this declaration, God spoke this word to Ezekiel as one of the compound names for God: *Jehovah-Shammah.*

Ezekiel was the priest-in-training who was deported to Babylon by the Chaldeans. This, of course, destroyed every hope he had cherished. There was no place for a priest to minister in captivity. On the very birthday when he should have been consecrated to the priesthood, God revealed Himself to Ezekiel and recommissioned him to be a prophet to the captives.

It may have seemed desirable to be commissioned into God's service, but Ezekiel didn't have the slightest idea of what it would entail. He became a demonstration of the prophecy God gave through him, telling his fellow captives of the impending destruction of Jerusalem. By divine command, he lived on starvation rations as a sign of the suffering the inhabitants of Jerusalem would experience, and there were long seasons when God prevented him from speaking to anyone unless there was a prophetic message from God. God denied Ezekiel the privilege of mourning when his wife died. This was a prophetic sign of the way Jerusalem's residents would behave during the fall of the Holy City.

During these seasons of visualized prophecy, God repeatedly gave Ezekiel visions. He saw the idolatry of the religious rulers in Jerusalem, and he saw the women worshiping the goddess of heaven instead of Jehovah. He felt the pain of God's heart, and he began to understand why God was sending His people into captivity.

In one of those visions, he saw the glory of Jehovah lift from the Holy of Holies and rest in the outer court, as though God said that those who ministered to God in the divine sanctuary no longer wanted that Presence, so God was making it available to the Levitical priests who could minister only in this outer court. The Levites must have ignored it, however, for soon Ezekiel saw the glory lift and move to the Mount of Olives. It rested there for a season as if to invite the common people to bask in God's Presence. When this did not occur, God lifted the cloud of His Presence into the heavens. Israel had lost the Presence of God.

God then opened Ezekiel's spiritual eyes to look into the future. He envisioned a magnificent Temple into which this glory returned, but it was unlike anything that has ever appeared on earth. Many generations later, Paul the Apostle said, "Do you not know that you are the temple of God and that the Spirit of God dwells in You?" and "You are the temple of the living God. As God has said: 'I will dwell in them and walk among them. I will be their God, and they shall be My people' " (1 Corinthians 3:16; 2 Corinthians 6:16).

Stripped of God's glory, deprived of God's Temple, and living under the chastening hand of Jehovah, Ezekiel ended his book looking into some glorious future day when Israel, released from captivity, had returned to her homeland. The past was disastrous, the future looked glorious; but what could Ezekiel expect in his immediate present?

The final statement of the book is a revelation of God so needed by those separated from everything they

considered holy. God told Ezekiel: *YHWH Shammah —
Jehovah-Shammah* — "THE LORD IS THERE" (Eze-
kiel 48:35). What a comfort this must have been to this
faithful prophet. To Ezekiel's pleading, "Where are you
LORD?" the answer was *Shammah* — "there."
" Where are you, LORD, when I am in captivity?"
Shammah — "there."

God was assuring Ezekiel that Jerusalem was not
the divine habitation. The capture of the city was not
tantamount to the loss of God, even though this was the
common projection of the nations around Israel. God
was with His covenant people wherever they went. He
once met them in the Temple. Now that the Temple no
longer existed, He offered to meet them in the brick
kilns. He lived with them in Jerusalem, now He lived
with them in Babylon. He was their God in freedom,
and He would equally be their God in captivity. By His
very nature, He is *Shammah* — "there."

Although this covenant name had not yet been
revealed to David, he entered into the reality of this
covenant. With great confidence he wrote, "God is our
refuge and strength, a very present help in trouble.
Therefore we will not fear, even though the earth be
removed, and though the mountains be carried into the
midst of the sea; though its waters roar and be troubled,
though the mountains shake with its swelling ... God is
in the midst ... God shall help ... The LORD of hosts is
with us; the God of Jacob is our refuge." Then David
ended his song with, "Be still, and know that I am God;
I will be exalted among the nations, I will be exalted in
the earth! The LORD of hosts is with us; the God of
Jacob is our refuge" (Psalm 46:1-3; 5,7; 10-11).

David could not visualize God as an absentee landlord. Jehovah was always present and often active in
the affairs of life. Long before David had erected his

humble Tabernacle as a repository for the Ark of the Covenant, he had a consciousness of the Presence of God. He regularly called upon *Jehovah-Shammah* for guidance, strength, and comfort. He even wrote, "When my father and my mother forsake me, then the LORD will take care of me" (Psalm 27:10).

David did not feel the need to await a special visitation of God to enjoy His Presence. He wrote, "As for me, I will call upon God, and the LORD shall save me. Evening and morning and at noon I will pray, and cry aloud, and He shall hear my voice" (Psalm 55:16-17), and, "Trust in Him at all times, you people; pour out your heart before Him; God is a refuge for us. Selah" (Psalm 62:8).

Jehovah-Shammah — "The Lord is There" — was a living reality to David. Since he worshiped a living God, it was natural to have His Presence always and everywhere. This released David to worship God always and everywhere.

It was the loss of the awareness of God's Presence that caused Israel to depart from worshiping Him. It is not true that absence makes the heart grow fonder, unless we add, "of someone else." As long as Solomon maintained a consciousness of God's Presence, he worshiped Jehovah with his whole heart. When he became rich and famous, his attention was diverted from Jehovah. His wives made him acutely aware of other gods, and his worship of Jehovah became cold and occasional. The Bible tells the story in this succinct statement: "For it was so, when Solomon was old, that his wives turned his heart after other gods; and his heart was not loyal to the LORD his God, as was the heart of his father David" (1 Kings 11:4). Subsequent kings had no consciousness of the living God whatsoever. They worshiped Baal and let the Temple of the

LORD fall into ruin. They forsook the Law of God and became a law unto themselves. The few kings of Judah who turned their hearts after God were consistently compared to David. He was the standard of God's desires. The Bible says, "Now the LORD was with Jehoshaphat, because he walked in the former ways of his father David; he did not seek the Baals" (2 Chronicles 17:3).

David's concept of a living God freed him from dividing life into the sacred and the secular. David preferred to see God involved in all the affairs of his existence, so one area was no more sacred than another. Of course, he enjoyed the Feast Days and the days of holy convocation where special emphasis was placed upon response to God, but David didn't view these times of his life as any more holy than when he was on the battlefield. In different ways, he worked with God in His plan for Israel.

David is gone, but his concepts remain. His form of worship is not acceptable to all Christians, but His God lives on. Cultures have evolved, and religion has greatly changed, but "Jesus Christ is the same yesterday, today, and forever" (Hebrews 13:8). David's Jehovah is Mary's Jesus.

CHAPTER 12

David's Jehovah
is Mary's Jesus

I AM!

"I am there" (*Jehovah-Shammah*) is the final Old Testament revelation of God's covenant, or compound, names. The New Testament begins with the announcement of the Angel of the Lord to Joseph that the Child to be born to Mary was to be called *Immanuel,* which means "God with us" (Matthew 1:23). Obviously, God's revelation was to be consistent and progressive. This is complementary to all good teaching. Instruction needs to move line upon line and precept upon precept (see Isaiah 28:10). It must progress from the seen to the unseen. John the Apostle reports, "There was a man of the Pharisees named Nicodemus, a ruler of the Jews. This man came to Jesus by night and said to Him, 'Rabbi, we know that You are a teacher come from God; for no one can do these signs that You do unless God is with him' " (John 3:1-2). "A teacher come from God" — there could be no higher credentials, for God is the ultimate Teacher. He graciously starts at the intellectual and experiential level of His pupils, and then He gently moves them step by step from the known to the unknown.

John introduces us to Jesus by saying, "In the beginning was the Word, and the Word was with God, and the Word was God" (John 1:1). This intertwines the written Word of God with the living Word. Jesus did not begin His teaching ministry after His baptism in the Jordan. He began His instruction as soon as He created the first man, Adam. God has continually sought to reveal His nature to mankind, and Jesus has been a constant channel of that revelation. In the Old Testament, His manifestation was as the "Angel of the LORD," while the Gospels call Him "Jesus" and the Epistles usually refer to Him as the "Christ." Having the same Teacher throughout human history has afforded us a consistent unfolding of truth about God.

The Bible Presents a Progressive Revelation of God

The covenant names of God that meant so much to David preceded and followed him. As I have suggested, David came to know some facets of God's nature before they were actually declared in written form, but this is not abnormal, for it was his relationship with God that gave him such advanced insights. We learn much from books, but we learn much more from a close relationship with the one about whom the books are written. What David learned and responded to did not cease with him. Many years after his death, prophets were experiencing those living truths about God, and some of them were expounding them with ardent zeal.

The revelation that God was *Jehovah-Jireh* began with Abraham, but God reaffirmed it again and again. For instance, when Elisha discovered that a prophet's widow was about to lose her two sons to slavery as payment to creditors, he embraced the revelation of *Jehovah-Jireh*. He instructed the widow to borrow every empty vessel her neighbors would loan to her, and pour into them the small oil supply she had in the house. The oil did not cease pouring until every pot and kettle was running over. Then Elisha told her to sell the oil, pay off her debts and live on the remaining money. She obeyed, and *Jireh* provided — "the LORD will provide!" What God had proclaimed as a definition now became definitive. He had supplied. This was not a single occurrence, for repeatedly God supplied what His chosen people needed.

The revelation of *Jehovah-Rapha* is equally progressive through the Bible. When the king of Syria learned that the God of Israel was a healing God, he sent his most trusted servant to the king of Israel with this note: " 'Now be advised, when this letter comes to you, that I have sent Naaman my servant to you, that you may heal him of his leprosy.' And it happened, when the king of Israel read the letter, that he tore his clothes and said, 'Am I God, to kill and make alive, that this man sends a man to me to heal him of his leprosy? Therefore please consider, and see how he seeks a quarrel with me' " (2 Kings 5:6-7). When Elisha heard of this problem in the palace, he sent for Naaman and instructed him, "Go and wash in the Jordan seven times, and your flesh shall be restored to you, and you shall be clean" (2 Kings 5:10). Reluctantly, Naaman obeyed, and God totally healed him. It was *Jehovah-Rapha* being Himself, the Healer.

Similarly, when King Hezekiah was sick and near death, the prophet Isaiah told him, "Thus says the LORD: 'Set your house in order, for you shall die, and not live' " (2 Kings 20:1). Hezekiah pled before the Lord

and wept bitterly, and God sent Isaiah back to the king
with the message, "Thus says the LORD, the God of
David your father: 'I have heard your prayer, I have
seen your tears; surely I will heal you. On the third day
you shall go up to the house of the LORD' " (2 Kings
20:5). Once again, the God Who established Himself as a
healing God at the waters of Marah functioned as
Jehovah-Rapha many generations later. The revelation
remained constant.

God's defensive nature as *Jehovah-Nissi* is equally
constant throughout the Old Testament. During
Jehoshaphat's reign in Judah, the kings of Moab,
Ammon and Syria united to invade Judah. When
Jehoshaphat cried out to the LORD and pled His
covenant promises to His people, saying, "Your name is
in this temple" (2 Chronicles 20:9), the LORD spoke
through a prophet saying, "Do not be afraid nor
dismayed because of this great multitude, for the battle
is not yours, but God's ... You will not need to fight in
this battle. Position yourselves, stand still and see the
salvation of the LORD, who is with you, O Judah and
Jerusalem!" (2 Chronicles 20:15-17).

At God's further command, the king "Appointed
those who should sing to the LORD, and who should
praise the beauty of holiness, as they went out before
the army and were saying: 'Praise the LORD, For His
mercy endures forever' " (2 Chronicles 20:21). God
preceded the praising choir and turned the enemy
against itself. Judah didn't have to lift a weapon in this
war, and it took them four days to collect all the spoil
from the slain enemy. *Jehovah-Nissi* had been their
complete defense.

This same witness applies to the other compound
names of God. The revelation of the divine character
unfolded in those names continued into succeeding

generations. *Jehovah-M'kaddesh* — the LORD our sanctification, or holiness — is heralded by the prophets. Isaiah calls the pathway of the redeemed "The Highway of Holiness" (Isaiah 35:8), and refers to God's power as "His holy arm" (Isaiah 52:10), while calling God's habitation "holy and glorious" (Isaiah 63:15).

God reaffirms the revelation of Himself as the source of our *peace* when the prophet writes, "The chastisement for our peace was upon Him, And by His stripes we are healed" (Isaiah 53:5). *Jehovah-Shalom* further states, " 'I create the fruit of the lips: Peace, peace to him who is far off and to him who is near,' says the LORD, 'And I will heal him' " (Isaiah 57:19). He also declared that the song Judah would sing in days to come would be: "You will keep him in perfect peace, Whose mind is stayed on You, Because he trusts in You" (Isaiah 26:3). Even the minor prophet, Haggai, quoted God as saying, "And in this place I will give peace" (Haggai 2:9). *Jehovah-Shalom* is far more than Gideon's concept of God. It is a facet of God's nature that will continue to unfold throughout all of time and eternity.

David loved to relate to Jehovah as *Rohi* — the Lord my Shepherd —but he wasn't alone in this vision of God. The prophet declared, "Behold, the LORD God shall come with a strong hand, And His arm shall rule for Him; Behold, His reward is with Him. He will feed His flock like a shepherd; He will gather the lambs with His arm, And carry them in His bosom, And gently lead those who are with young" (Isaiah 40:10-11). In the same passage of Scripture the scribes quoted to the Wise Men when asked where the Messiah was to be born, the prophet adds, "He shall stand and feed His flock In the strength of the LORD, In the majesty of the name of the LORD His God; And they shall abide, For now He shall be great to the ends of the earth; And this One shall be peace" (Micah 5:4-5). The concept of God as Shepherd and Peace continued to the end of the Old Testament.

In a similar manner, the revelation of *Jehovah-Tsidkenu* — the LORD our Righteousness — is progressive. In the poetic description of the death of Jesus, Isaiah adds, "He shall see the labor of His soul, and be satisfied. By His knowledge My righteous Servant shall justify many, For He shall bear their iniquities" (Isaiah 53:11). That God is righteous is an accepted norm, but *Tsidkenu* declares that God has become *our* righteousness. This was difficult for those under the Law to understand, but God said it again and again until those who came to know Him could grasp it for themselves. *Tsidkenu* — "My righteous Servant shall justify many, For He shall bear their iniquities." In this, the nature of God and the mission of Christ are blended. Christ imputes some of His nature to us.

The last compound name for Jehovah came to Ezekiel as the final word of his prophetic book: *Shammah* — "The LORD is there" (Ezekiel 48:35). Hundreds of persons experienced the reality of that in the years that followed, but none had a more dramatic example of it than did Shadrach, Meshach, and Abed-Nego, the three Hebrew children. Cast into a super-heated furnace of fire for their refusal to worship Nebuchadnezzar's golden image, they were joined by *Jehovah-Shammah* in such a visible way that the king exclaimed, "Look! ... I see four men loose, walking in the midst of the fire; and they are not hurt, and the form of the fourth is like the Son of God ... there is no other God who can deliver like this" (Daniel 3:25,29). This manifestation of the Presence of God caused this Babylonian king to issue a proclamation of the greatness of Jehovah in which he "blessed the Most High and praised and honored Him who lives forever: For His dominion is an everlasting dominion, And His kingdom is from generation to generation" (Daniel 4:34).

The most lasting demonstration of the greatness of God is His divine Presence among His people. Self-revelation is a perpetual desire of God. To His covenant people, He said, "I will betroth you to Me forever; yes, I will betroth you to Me In righteousness and justice, In lovingkindness and mercy. I will betroth you to Me in faithfulness, And *you shall know the LORD*" (Hosea 2:19-20, emphasis added). He also said, "For I desire ... the knowledge of God more than burnt offerings" (Hosea 6:6). How deceived we are to believe that God wants things or service from us. His expressed desire is that we come to know Him. Giving and serving are merely means to an end, but that end is the knowledge of God and the intimate fellowship this will release. As long as there is time, there will be a continual unfolding of the nature of God to seeking men and women.

Jesus is the New Testament Revelation of the Nature of God

Although several hundred years passed between the writing of the last book of the Old Testament and the compiling of the first book of the New Testament, the message remains consistent. God is revealing Himself. Jesus came as our *Immanuel* — "God with us." Early in His ministry, He told the scribes and Pharisees, who were the religious leaders of the day, "If God were your Father, you would love Me, for I proceeded forth and came from God; nor have I come of Myself, but He sent Me" (John 8:42). Their defense was: "Abraham is our father" (John 8:39). Jesus told them, "Your father Abraham rejoiced to see My day, and he saw it and was glad ... Most assuredly, I say to you, before Abraham was, I AM" (John 8:56,58). This claim of Jesus to be the *Jehovah* — the I AM — so angered these leaders that "they took up stones to throw at Him; but Jesus hid Himself and went out of the temple" (John 8:59).

Many years later, while the author of this Gospel was on the prison island of Patmos, he was given a dramatic revelation of Jesus Christ in which Jesus in heaven proclaimed, "I am the Alpha and the Omega, the Beginning and the End ... who is and who was and who is to come, the Almighty. I am He who lives, and was dead, and behold, I am alive forevermore. Amen" (Revelation 1:8,18). The *I AM* Who spoke to Moses at the burning bush is now among people in human flesh. The Gospel of John gives us at least seven similes to His *I AM* nature. "I am the bread of life" (John 6:35); "I am the light of the world" (8:12); "I am the good shepherd" (10:11); "I am the way, the truth, and the life" (14:6) and "I am the true vine" (15:1). There can be no mistaking this message: *Jesus* in the New Testament equals *Jehovah* in the Old Testament; they are the same. God clothed with majesty in the covenant of Law became God clothed with human flesh in the covenant of Grace to reveal the majesty of God to sinful persons. Each of the compound, covenant names of God is fully manifested in the life, ministry and message of Jesus Christ.

Jesus-Jireh

That Jesus is *Jehovah-Jireh* — our Provider — is proved by Christ's miracles of supply. It was *Jireh* Who turned water into wine for the wedding at Cana of Galilee. He needed but a few fish and loaves of bread to feed 5,000 men plus the women and the children on one occasion and 4,000 or more persons at another time. Jesus more than demonstrated that He was our Source of provision; He also declared it. He told His disciples, "Whatever you ask in My name, that I will do, that the Father may be glorified in the Son. If you ask anything in My name, I will do it" (John 14:13-14). He further stated, "If you abide in Me, and My words abide in you, you will ask what you desire, and it shall be done for you" (John 15:7). To a much broader audience, Jesus said, "Ask, and it will be given to you; seek, and you will find; knock, and it will be opened to you. For everyone who asks receives, and he who seeks finds, and to him who knocks it will be opened" (Matthew 7:7-8). Jesus was announcing that *Jehovah-Jireh* was "open for business." God's source of supply was among His people, and, as Paul later wrote, "My God shall supply all your need according to His riches in glory by Christ Jesus" (Philippians 4:19). God is the *Source;* our need determines the *product;* God's divine riches are the *limitations,* and Christ Jesus is the *Agent* that brings this all together. Could God have more clearly defined His giving nature than in sending His Son to display and disclose it to us?

Jesus-Rapha

Only the person who has never read the Gospels would fail to see Jesus as a glorious demonstration of *Jehovah-Rapha* — the Lord our Healer. We could so easily ask the woman who Jesus healed from years of hemorrhaging to be a witness for Him. She touched only the hem of Christ's garment, but with this healing God accomplished instantly what doctors had been unable to do in twelve years (see Matthew 9:20-22). Or perhaps the centurion would testify to Christ's healing power, for Jesus healed his servant with a simple command (see Matthew 8:5-13). The lepers that Jesus cleansed and the persons delivered from evil spirits would stand in line to declare that Jesus was, indeed, *Jehovah-Rapha* — the God Who had healed them.

That this manifestation of the nature of God did not cease when Christ was resurrected and ascended to the Father is made clear by the healing ministry of the saints in the book of Acts and by the statement of James, "The prayer of faith will save the sick, and the Lord will raise him up" (James 5:15). Jesus, Who was the healing God, now *is* the healing God, for "Jesus Christ is the same yesterday, today, and forever" (Hebrews 13:8).

Jesus-Nissi

Jehovah-Nissi — our Banner, our Protector — is characterized in Jesus. He showed Himself to be our Defender against death by raising the widow's son in the midst of the funeral procession and in raising Lazarus after he had been in the grave for three days. In heaven He declared, "I am alive forevermore. Amen. And I have the keys of Hades and of Death" (Revelation 1:18). Since He controls the locks, no one else controls our lives. Furthermore, Jesus gave His disciples "power and authority over all demons, and to cure diseases" (Luke 9:1), and before His ascension into heaven, He testified, "All authority has been given to Me in heaven and on earth. Go therefore and make disciples of all the nations, baptizing them in the name of the Father and of the Son and of the Holy Spirit, teaching them to observe all things that I have commanded you; and lo, I am with you always, even to the end of the age" (Matthew 28:19-20). He conferred His authority upon us, and then promised to be with us as surely as the banner was with Israel in the midst of her battles. *Jehovah-Nissi*, in the person of Jesus Christ, still defends His people and goes before them in time of battle.

Jesus-M'kaddesh

Jesus is equally our *Jehovah-M'kaddesh*, our sanctification. In my earlier book, *Let Us Be Holy*, I wrote: "That Jesus was indeed the Holy One of God was demonstrated repeatedly during His lifetime. At His baptism, John declared, ' ... This is the Son of God' (John 1:34); during His ministry, demons declared Him to be '... The Holy One of God' (Luke 4:34), and the early Church prayed, '... That signs and wonders may be done by the name of Thy Holy Child Jesus' (Acts 4:30). At Jesus' death, the centurion who supervised the crucifixion declared, 'Truly this Man was the Son of God' (Mark 15:39), and in Christ's resurrection His holiness was finally confirmed once and for all. David had prophesied, and Peter and Paul quoted it, '... Thou shalt not suffer thine Holy One to see corruption' (Psalm 16:10; Acts 2:27; 13:35). Christ's resurrection as the first fruits of the Church proved incontestably that He was the Holy One, the One in Whom was inherent holiness ... Christ was not only the Holy One of God, but was the Sent One from God. Christ was sent from God, not as a prophet with a message from God, but to demonstrate, display, and reveal the Father. He had more than a ministry to share; He had a divine nature to show. After all, He was and is God; the Father and Son share the same nature. Jesus attested to this repeatedly in the Gospel of John" (pages 29-30).

Jesus-Shalom

As the demonstrator of the nature of God, Jesus was certainly *Jehovah-Shalom* — the Lord our Peace. At the birth of Jesus, the angels announced to the shepherds on Bethlehem's hillside, "On earth peace ...

toward men" (Luke 2:14). The coming of Christ was the automatic coming of peace, for He is the Prince of Peace. What peace and calm He displayed in the midst of His enemies, in the presence of demonic activity, in the sinking boat on Galilee, and among His disciples. Nothing threatened His calm assurance of the perfect will of the Father. Before entering the garden of Gethsemane, Jesus told the disciples, "Peace I leave with you, My peace I give to you; not as the world gives do I give to you. Let not your heart be troubled, neither let it be afraid" (John 14:27). From a Roman jail cell, the Apostle Paul wrote, "For He Himself is our peace, who has made both one, and has broken down the middle wall of separation" (Ephesians 2:14). Jesus Christ came into our world both to exemplify and to extend God's peace to enable us to be at rest with God and in harmony one with another. *Shalom!*

Jesus-Rohi

How David loved the revelation of *Jehovah-Rohi* — the Lord my Shepherd. It is obvious that Jesus loved it, too, for He shared a lengthy discourse on this. In His talk, He said two times, "I am the good shepherd" (John 10:11,14). He spoke of Himself as being the "door of the sheep" (John 10:7), and He declared that His sheep would not follow a stranger. He said that He knew His sheep and that they knew Him. Contrasting Himself to a hireling, He declared His readiness to lay down His life for His sheep.

Everything that David envisioned in the shepherding care of Jehovah, Jesus declared He had come to do. Many years later, Peter spoke of Jesus as "The Chief Shepherd" (1 Peter 5:4), and so He remains to His Church. *Jehovah-Rohi* still carries the lambs in His bosom, binds up the wounded, calms the fearful, feeds the hungry, waters the thirsty, and helps with the lambing. Many Christians have responded to Jesus with David's concept of God: "Yea, though I walk through the valley of the shadow of death, I will fear no evil; For You are with me; Your rod and Your staff, they comfort me" (Psalm 23:4).

Jesus-Tsidkenu

New Testament believers have come to learn there is no righteousness acceptable in God's Presence other than the righteousness of Jesus Christ, Who has become to us *Jehovah-Tsidkenu* — the Lord our Righteousness. Paul beautifully summed this up in his letter to the Romans, where he wrote, "There is therefore now no condemnation to those who are in Christ Jesus, who do not walk according to the flesh, but according to the Spirit ... For what the law could not do in that it was weak through the flesh, God did by sending His own Son in the likeness of sinful flesh, on account of sin: He condemned sin in the flesh, that the righteous requirement of the law might be fulfilled in us who do not walk according to the flesh but according to the Spirit" (Romans 8:1,3-4). Paul also wrote, "For as by one man's disobedience many were made sinners, so also by one Man's obedience many will be made righteous" (Romans 5:19). Perhaps Christ's vicarious righteousness is best summed up: "For He made Him who knew no sin to be sin for us, that we might become the righteousness of God in Him" (2 Corinthians 5:21). Blessed *Tsidkenu!*

Jesus-Shammah

Jesus Himself taught us that He is our *Jehovah-Shammah.* He related, "Where two or three are gathered together in My name, I am there in the midst of them" (Matthew 18:20). The recurring theme of the New Testament is "Christ in you." God, Who dwelt among His people in the Old Testament, dwells in the New Testament believers. The finished work of Christ's cross makes this possible, for sin has been put away and the Holy Spirit has come to reside. *Jehovah-Shammah* is as real to believers as the breath they breathe. Every revelation of God's name given to us in the Old Testament finds expression in the God-man Who came to bring us into the Presence of God Almighty. Jesus and Jehovah are but different manifestations of the one LORD. He lived, and He lives! David's God is certainly our God.

CHAPTER 13

David's God is Our God

It would be foolish to even imply that David stood alone in his revelation of a living God. The Bible tells us of many Old Testament characters who also lived in that glorious awareness. They were a pitiful minority and most of them were viewed as seers, mystics, or prophets. They frequently lived secluded lives and they were often quite out of touch with society.

David just didn't fit this pattern. He didn't need the incantations of the mystics or the special prayer places of the prophets. David was a king, warrior, husband and father. He was constantly in touch with society, but he never lost touch with God. He, as we, lived in a time/space capsule, but he had eternity in his heart. The unseen God had a tug on his heartstrings somewhat like the tug of a kite flying above low-hanging clouds.

David's uniqueness lies less in his awareness of a living God and more in what he did with that perception. He was not a private man. David lived out loud. He hurled his convictions at others in teaching, demonstrating, songs and Psalms. He seemed convinced that what he had learned about God should be shared with everyone on the earth. He used his position as king to make the reality of Jehovah real to all the subjects of his domain.

To the day of his death, David never lost the awareness of a living God. This was not true of the kings who followed him. His son, Solomon, began with this same awareness, but as wealth and fame came to him, God seemed more and more distant. The Bible records: "When Solomon was old ... his wives turned his heart after other gods; and his heart was not loyal to the LORD his God, as was the heart of his father David" (1 Kings 11:4).

Subsequent kings, like many Americans, rarely possessed an awareness of a living God. Whenever this conviction is lost, worship ceases and evil reigns. Israel's kings worshiped Baal, burned their children as sacrifices to Molech, abandoned the Law of God and let the Temple of the Lord fall into ruin. Americans have their own idols: we sacrifice our children in abortion; substitute TV for the Bible, and forsake our churches. They could not be stopped, and neither can we; for whenever we abandon the Law of God, we become a law unto ourselves.

God did not see David as an exception. He chose him as a model. From time to time, a king in Judah would turn to the Lord, and he would be compared to David. Of Jehoshaphat, the Bible testifies, "Now the LORD was with Jehoshaphat, because he walked in the former ways of his father David; he did not seek the Baals" (2 Chronicles 17:3). God used David as a standard by which He judged other leaders.

Generations after David wrote his last Psalm, One far greater than David came on the scene. This Man not only believed in a living God, He *was* the living God.

The Apostle John testified, "The Word became flesh and dwelt among us, and we beheld His glory, the glory as of the only begotten of the Father, full of grace and truth" (John 1:14). He came to reveal the Father to us in word, deed, and attitude. "Jesus said ... 'He who has seen Me has seen the Father' " (John 14:9). David's theme became the theme of Christ: God is alive! Jesus testified before His Father's throne, "I am He who lives, and was dead, and behold, I am alive forevermore. Amen" (Revelation 1:18). Eventually, this became the theme of the disciples.

The Theme of the Apostles is "Christ is Alive"

As the divine ministry of Christ Jesus continued to unfold before the eyes of the disciples, their confidence in Him crystallized. Peter, in answer to Christ's question, " 'Who do men say that I, the Son of Man, am," declared: " 'You are the Christ, the Son of the living God.' Jesus answered and said to him, 'Blessed are you, Simon Bar-Jonah, for flesh and blood has not revealed this to you, but My Father who is in heaven' " (Matthew 16:13,16-17). Christ promised to build His Church upon this confession. From this point on, the disciples saw Jesus in quite a different light. They began to make concrete plans to reign with Him in His kingdom.

All of these concepts perished like paper in a fire when Jesus hung His head on the cross and cried, " 'It is finished!' And bowing His head, He gave up His spirit" (John 19:30). The disciples were absolutely convinced that it was finished. Fearfully, they returned to the Upper Room and locked themselves in. Christ was dead, and all of their hopes had died with Him.

On that first Easter morning, when the two Marys came to the Upper Room to report their discovery of an empty tomb, hope began to revive among these despondent men. Later, Peter and John verified this report, and when two of the disciples who had returned to Emmaus told of having walked with Jesus on the road, they began to recall Christ's teachings that He would rise from the dead on the third day. This was that day! When Jesus Himself entered their locked room and ate with them, their last doubts disappeared, and joyfully they reached out anew to the life that they thought was lost forever. In the three short days between the crucifixion and the resurrection of Jesus, these disciples learned what religion has failed to grasp in the hundreds of years that have followed: memories of what Jesus was and what He did are insufficient grounds for saving faith. Whenever we lose the awareness that Christ is a *living God,* faith declines, fear amplifies, and defeat is inevitable. Peter, who lived through this terrifying experience, wrote: "Blessed be the God and Father of our Lord Jesus Christ, who according to His abundant mercy has begotten us again to a living hope through the resurrection of Jesus Christ from the dead" (1 Peter 1:3).

Peter Embraced a Living God

Peter was the first of the disciples to proclaim publicly the message of the living God. On the day of Pentecost, he stood to address the bewildered assembly of Jews from many provinces and countries who had come to Jerusalem for the Feast and had witnessed the results of the coming of the Holy Spirit upon the 120 who had assembled in the Upper Room. In his explanatory sermon, Peter declared: "Men of Israel, hear these words: Jesus of Nazareth, a Man attested by God to you by miracles, wonders, and signs which God did through Him in your midst, as you yourselves also know — Him, being delivered by the determined purpose and foreknowledge of God, you have taken by lawless hands, have crucified, and put to death; whom God raised up, having loosed the pains of death, because it was not possible that He should be held by it" (Acts 2:22-24).

Peter was proclaiming a living God to the very people who had contributed to the death of Jesus Christ. Reaching beyond the testimony of personal experience, Peter quoted from the Psalter, "For David says concerning Him: 'I foresaw the LORD always before my face, For He is at my right hand, that I may not be shaken. Therefore my heart rejoiced, and my tongue was glad; Moreover my flesh also will rest in hope. For You will not leave my soul in Hades, Nor will You allow Your Holy One to see corruption. You have made known to me the ways of life; You will make me full of joy in Your Presence' " (Acts 2:25-28). David worshiped a living God, and Peter had come to worship that same living God.

When the Lord lowered a sheet filled with cere-monially unclean animals and commanded Peter to eat them, this disciple interpreted the vision to be a challenge to share the message of a living God with the Gentiles. Because of this, he accompanied the waiting soldiers from the Caesarean centurion and preached Christ Jesus to the household of Cornelius. In this address, he said, "Him [Jesus] God raised up on the third day, and showed Him openly, not to all the people, but to witnesses chosen before by God, even to us who ate and drank with Him after He arose from the dead. And He commanded us to preach to the people, and to testify that it is He who was ordained by God to be Judge of the living and the dead" (Acts 10:40-42). The reality of a living God became so powerful that Cornel-ius and his entire household not only believed, but were filled with the Holy Spirit. Before the evening was over, Peter baptized all of them in water.

Peter preached the resurrection of Jesus so boldly and openly that the religious leaders had him arrested on several occasions. When they pressured King Herod to arrest him, he sentenced Peter to death; but the night before his scheduled execution, an angel of the Lord brought him out of prison in a supernatural escape. Peter testified to the event and said, "Now I know for certain that the Lord has sent His angel, and has delivered me from the hand of Herod and from all the expectation of the Jewish people," and when he reported this to the believers who had been praying for his release, "He declared to them how the Lord had brought him out of the prison" (Acts 12:11,17).

Peter immediately credited the entire episode to the intervention of the living God as seen in Christ Jesus. The resurrection of Jesus was no more a doctrine to Peter than it had been to David. It was a living reality!

Stephen Espoused a Living God

The first martyr of the early Church was a deacon named Stephen, a man "full of faith and power, [who] did great wonders and signs among the people" (Acts 6:8). He was, obviously, a preaching deacon, and his preaching about a living Christ was too disturbing to the Jewish community. "They were not able to resist the wisdom and the Spirit by which he spoke" (Acts 6:10). The religious leaders brought false charges against Stephen, and in his defense, he began with Abraham and briefly recounted the history of Israel through the resurrection of Christ Jesus. He repeatedly emphasized the intervention of a living God into the affairs of His chosen race. It so angered the listeners that they did not wait for the vote of the council. "When they heard these things they were cut to the heart, and they gnashed at him with their teeth. But he, being full of the Holy Spirit, gazed into heaven and saw the glory of God, and Jesus standing at the right hand of God, and said, 'Look! I see the heavens opened and the Son of Man standing at the right hand of God!' " This was too much for the Jews, "and they cast him out of the city and stoned him. And the witnesses laid down their clothes at the feet of a young man named Saul" (Acts 7:54-56, 58). The last words of this godly man declared that Jesus was alive and well in the heavens. His last words were, "Look! I see the heavens opened and the Son of Man standing at the right hand of God!" (Acts 7:56). A living Christ stood waiting to receive His martyr into the heavens. What does the pain of thrown stones matter when the living God stands waiting to greet you?

Paul Expounded a Living God

The man who held the coats of the witnesses to the stoning of Stephen was Saul of Tarsus, whose name God changed to Paul. The testimony of Stephen was so overwhelming to Saul that he responded with vehement anger against the believers in Jesus. He tortured, maimed, killed and imprisoned many of them. As he was armed with religious authority to persecute the Church in the region of Damascus in a similar manner, God intercepted Saul with a bright light from heaven. "Then he fell to the ground, and heard a voice saying to him 'Saul, Saul, why are you persecuting Me?' And he said, 'Who are You, Lord?' Then the Lord said, 'I am Jesus, whom you are persecuting. It is hard for you to kick against the goads' " (Acts 9:4-5).

This dramatic conversion experience totally transformed Saul's thinking. His theological training under

Gamaliel needed the post graduate training that could come from none other than a living God. Once Saul knew that Jesus was alive, and that He was indeed God, everything changed. The persecutor became a severely persecuted preacher for his blazing messages on the resurrection of Jesus. On a missionary journey that brought him to Athens, Paul went to the Areopagus, where the Greek philosophers gathered to discuss the meaning of life. "Then certain Epicurean and Stoic philosophers encountered him. And some said, 'What does this babbler want to say?' Others said, 'He seems to be a proclaimer of foreign gods,' because he preached to them Jesus and the resurrection" (Acts 17:18). Paul took as his text an inscription he had read on one of their altars: "TO THE UNKNOWN GOD." "Therefore, the One whom you worship without knowing, Him I proclaim to you: 'God, who made the world and everything in it, since He is Lord of heaven and earth, does not dwell in temples made with hands. Nor is He worshiped with men's hands, as though He needed anything, since He gives to all life, breath, and all things ... He has appointed a day on which He will judge the world in righteousness by the Man whom He has ordained. He has given assurance of this to all by raising Him from the dead.' And when they heard of the resurrection of the dead, some mocked, while others said, 'We will hear you again on this matter' " (Acts 17:23-25, 31-32). Paul proclaimed a living God Who was as involved with the lives of these Athenians as He had been with the life of David.

Paul was powerful in his argument for the resurrection of Christ and His living availability. He used the Law and the Prophets, and quoted widely from David's Psalms. He referred to eye witnesses, and three times, in major defenses, he recounted his conversion experience as proof positive that Jesus was alive and very interested in His Church. Unable to successfully counter Paul's arguments, his Jewish listeners reacted in violent anger. They beat Paul, stoned him, frequently imprisoned him and at least once threw him to the lions. Paul's worst attack came in the Temple in Jerusalem, where the Jews caused such an uproar that Roman soldiers were dispatched to prevent Paul's murder in the Temple.

Paul was allowed to plead a defense before the High Priest, Ananias. "When Paul perceived that one part was Sadducees and the other Pharisees, he cried out in the council, 'Men and brethren, I am a Pharisee, the son of a Pharisee; concerning the hope and resurrection of the dead I am being judged!' " (Acts 23:6). This divided the council so that instead of making a decision, they returned Paul to the Roman government for trial.

Five days later, the council reconvened with the Roman governor, Felix, as the judge. After the prosecuting attorney, Tertullus, finished his arguments against Paul, Felix gave Paul permission to defend himself. Paul said, "I have hope in God, which they themselves also accept, that there will be a resurrection of the dead, both of the just and the unjust." Then Paul professed ignorance of the charges against him: "Unless it is for this one statement which I cried out, standing among them, 'Concerning the resurrection of the dead I am being judged by you this day' " (Acts 24:15,21).

Later, when Paul presented his defense before King Agrippa and Festus, he said, "Therefore, having obtained help from God, to this day I stand, witnessing both to small and great, saying no other things than those which the prophets and Moses said would come — that Christ would suffer, that He would be the first to rise from the dead, and would proclaim light to the Jewish people and to the Gentiles" (Acts 26:22-23).

This was the theme of Paul's messages: Jesus is alive, and we shall live with Him. He wrote, "But now Christ is risen from the dead, and has become the firstfruits of those who have fallen asleep" (1 Corinthians 15:20). Paul, like David, earnestly believed in a living God.

James Exemplified a Living God

All who wrote the books of the New Testament gave testimony to Jesus, the living God. *James* says that we can "draw near" to God (4:8), and that we live in the "sight of God" (4:10). He even tempers the behavior of Christians by saying, "if the Lord wills" (4:15). In light of the reality of a living God, he urges us, "Therefore be patient, brethren, until the coming of the Lord ... Establish your hearts, for the coming of the Lord is at hand" (5:7-8). James so lived in the awareness of a living God that it affected his present behavior and his future plans.

John Experienced a Living God

The entire theme of John's first epistle is the wonder of serving a living God. His prologue sets the theme: "That which was from the beginning, which we have heard, which we have seen with our eyes, which we have looked upon, and our hands have handled, concerning the Word of life — the life was manifested, and we have seen, and bear witness and declare to you that eternal life which was with the Father and was manifested to us — that which we have seen and heard we declare to you, that you also may have fellowship with us; and truly our fellowship is with the Father and with His Son Jesus Christ. And these things we write to you that your joy may be full" (1 John 1:1-4). Then John speaks of our enjoying fellowship with Christ (1 John 1:7), and of abiding in Him (2:28). He even asserts:

"Beloved, now we are children of God; and it has not yet been revealed what we shall be, but we know that when He is revealed, we shall be like Him, for we shall see Him as He is" (1 John 3:2). John believed in a living God in a most practical way.

We, Too, May Worship a Living God

David worshiped a living God, Whom he knew as Jehovah, or the Almighty. Much later, Jesus came as the personification of Jehovah, declaring Himself to be the "I AM" — He Who met Moses at the burning bush. In accepting Jesus as the Messiah, the disciples had the most perfect manifestation of a living God that anyone had ever experienced. They walked, talked, ate, and ministered with the living God Who had become flesh to dwell among them.

When Christ's resurrection followed His crucifixion, these men invested the rest of their natural lives in proclaiming throughout their known world the reality of a living God. What they knew became the basis of a living, vibrant faith that motivated everything they said and did. They lived transformed lives, because they had moved from the ritual of the Temple to the reality of the Christ. Religion was replaced with reality, and a Person, Jesus, replaced mere principles and precepts.

It is to be expected, then, that their writings would encourage a similar faith in modern believers. We have been called, not so much to a faith in the continuity of religion, as we have been challenged to the continuation of a relationship with the living God. Paul taught, "Christ in you, the hope of glory" (Colossians 1:27). John verified Paul's teaching by saying, "This is the testimony: that God has given us eternal life, and this life is in His Son. He who has the Son has life; he who does not have the Son of God does not have life" (1 John 5:11-12).

The New Testament more than teaches the reality of a living God. In Christ Jesus, it affirms that this living God, through the agency of His Spirit, actually indwells the believers of this generation. Because of this, we can have a worship that is as vibrant as that of the disciples. Since pure worship is a loving response to a living God, the more complete our awareness of this living God, the higher our love responses will rise in worship. This is why the Bible has been given to us: to cause us to know the living God. John closed his Gospel by saying, "These things are written that you may believe that Jesus is the Christ, the Son of God, and that believing you may have life in His name" (John 20:31). When this living God makes His abode in our hearts, we will join David in singing, "O LORD, our Lord, How excellent is Your name in all the earth!" (Psalm 8:9).